FOR TEEN GIRLS

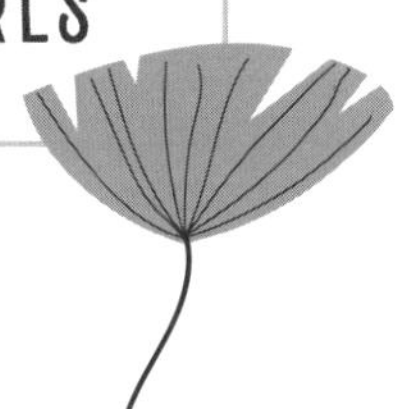

JOANNE SIMMONS

quiet-time devotions FOR TEEN GIRLS

180 DAYS OF
COMFORTING INSPIRATION

BARBOUR
PUBLISHING

Print ISBN 979-8-89151-028-9

Cover Design: Greg Jackson, Thinkpen Design

Published by Barbour Publishing, Inc., 1810 Barbour Drive, Uhrichsville, Ohio 44683, www.barbourbooks.com

Our mission is to inspire the world with the life-changing message of the Bible.

Printed in China.

INTRODUCTION

So many people and things want you to pay attention *right now*. Can you relate? Your parents, loved ones, teachers, coaches, and bosses want your attention, of course. And your friends, television, phone, laptop, social media, and homework all want you to pay attention too. All this can make life too loud and overwhelming sometimes! So you have to take time to be quiet—especially by focusing on the one true God who created you on purpose and loves you like crazy. The more quiet time you spend with Him, the more you learn about Him, the more you find out His good plans for your life, and the more you are filled with His love, wisdom, comfort, and peace!

Strengthen your relationship with the heavenly Father as you read through these devotions and prayers designed to help you grow deeper in your faith. Each inspiring, comforting reading will encourage you to bask in the blessing of personal quiet time with the one who loves you most.

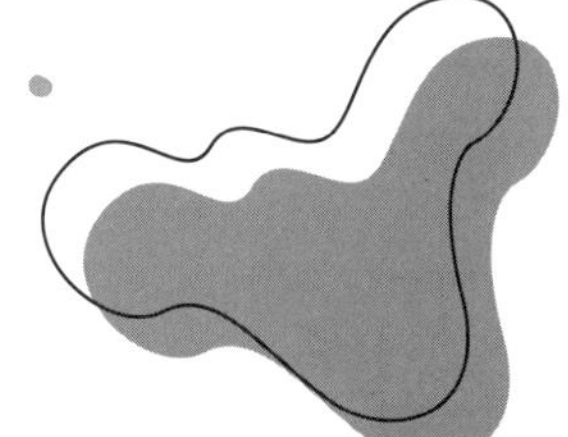

WHAT DOES IT MATTER? PART 1

We are made right with God by placing our faith in Jesus Christ. And this is true for everyone who believes, no matter who we are. For everyone has sinned; we all fall short of God's glorious standard. Yet God, in his grace, freely makes us right in his sight. He did this through Christ Jesus when he freed us from the penalty for our sins. For God presented Jesus as the sacrifice for sin. People are made right with God when they believe that Jesus sacrificed his life, shedding his blood. This sacrifice shows that God was being fair when he held back and did not punish those who sinned in times past, for he was looking ahead and including them in what he would do in this present time. God did this to demonstrate his righteousness, for he himself is fair and just, and he makes sinners right in his sight when they believe in Jesus.

Romans 3:22–26 NLT

What does it matter whether you spend quiet time with God? It matters—a lot!—because how you relate to God is the most important thing about you. Whether or not you have a relationship with God affects every area of your life in this world—and in your eternal life. So, do you have a relationship with God?

DEAR GOD, I WANT TO BE 100 PERCENT SURE OF MY RELATIONSHIP WITH YOU. AMEN.

WHAT DOES IT MATTER? PART 2

For God so loved the world that he gave his one and only Son, that whoever believes in him shall not perish but have eternal life.

JOHN 3:16 NIV

You need to know this about having a relationship with God: He created everything, including the first people, Adam and Eve. But when they chose to disobey the good instructions He gave them, they sinned, and that sin spread everywhere and put every awful thing into the world. But there's good news! God made a way to conquer sin and death and provide life that lasts forever through relationship with Him. The way is Jesus!

God showed the awesome love He has for all people by giving His only Son, Jesus Christ, to die to pay the price of sin for every single person who truly trusts in Him. And then Jesus rose from the dead, proving God's power over death—power that He gives to us when we accept Jesus as the only Savior from our sin.

DEAR GOD, I'M SO HAPPY AND GRATEFUL THAT YOU SENT JESUS AS THE WAY, THE TRUTH, AND THE LIFE (JOHN 14:6)! AMEN.

WHAT DOES IT MATTER? PART 3

God showed how much he loved us by sending his one and only Son into the world so that we might have eternal life through him. This is real love—not that we loved God, but that he loved us and sent his Son as a sacrifice to take away our sins.

1 John 4:9–10 NLT

There is no better quiet-time prayer than something like this:

> *Dear God, I know I make bad choices that go against Your good ways sometimes, so I know I'm a sinner. Please forgive me. I trust that You sent Your Son, Jesus Christ, as the only Savior from sin. I believe Jesus died on the cross to pay for my sin and that He rose again and gives me life that lasts forever. I want to give my life to You, God, and do my best to live like Jesus. I love You, and I need Your help in everything I think and say and do. Amen.*

If you've prayed this prayer and really, truly mean it, then you have a relationship with God and life that lasts forever—and *nothing* and *no one* can ever take those away from you!

DEAR GOD, THANK YOU THAT I AM SAVED FOREVER BECAUSE OF JESUS, AND I AM YOUR CHILD NOW AND EVERY DAY TO COME—FOR ETERNITY! AMEN.

TRUE FRIEND FOREVER

The truth is the Good News. When you heard the truth, you put your trust in Christ. Then God marked you by giving you His Holy Spirit as a promise. The Holy Spirit was given to us as a promise that we will receive everything God has for us. God's Spirit will be with us until God finishes His work of making us complete.

EPHESIANS 1:13–14 NLV

Once you've asked Jesus to be your Savior, you have the closest kind of friend who will never leave you and will always help you. That friend is God's Holy Spirit. God wants you to spend some quiet time focusing on His Holy Spirit, who is now within you. He wants you to hang out with Him. He sees all and knows all and loves you even more than all the people on earth who love you best. He is the very best friend to get to know and grow closer to.

DEAR GOD, THANK YOU FOR THE HOLY SPIRIT AND FOR BEING MY CLOSEST, TRUEST FRIEND. I WANT TO KNOW YOU BETTER AND BETTER EACH DAY. AMEN.

THE TWO MOST IMPORTANT COMMANDS

One of the teachers of the law. . .asked, "Of all the commandments, which is the most important?" Jesus replied, "The most important commandment is this: 'Listen, O Israel! The Lord *our God is the one and only* Lord. *And you must love the* Lord *your God with all your heart, all your soul, all your mind, and all your strength.' The second is equally important: 'Love your neighbor as yourself.' No other commandment is greater than these."*

Mark 12:28–31 NLT

The most important things Jesus asks of us are these: First, love God with everything that is in you—all your heart, soul, mind, and strength; and second, love your neighbor (anyone around you) the same as you love yourself.

You've probably heard some people say, "Jesus just says to love everyone. That's all you must do." But they often ignore the fact that He said *before* we love others, we are to love God first and most of all. We can't love others in the best ways that God intended unless we first love Him with all our heart, soul, mind, and strength—and that includes getting to know Him through His Word and through prayer.

DEAR JESUS, I WANT TO FOLLOW YOUR GREATEST COMMANDMENTS TO LOVE YOU FIRST AND THEN LOVE OTHERS. PLEASE KEEP TEACHING ME HOW. AMEN.

HAVE YOU BEEN BAPTIZED?

One day when the crowds were being baptized, Jesus himself was baptized. As he was praying, the heavens opened, and the Holy Spirit, in bodily form, descended on him like a dove. And a voice from heaven said, "You are my dearly loved Son, and you bring me great joy."

LUKE 3:21–22 NLT

If you have accepted Jesus as your Savior, have you been baptized? It's not something you absolutely have to do to be saved and go to heaven forever. The man who died next to Jesus when He died on the cross never had a chance to be baptized, and Jesus promised the man he would be with Him that day in paradise (Luke 23:42–43). But if you do have a chance, it's a blessing to obey God's Word and follow Jesus' example.

Baptism is a symbol with water to represent washing away your sin and choosing new life with Jesus. It helps show that you want to obey God and do your best to be like Jesus, and that you are saved from sin and are His follower.

HEAVENLY FATHER, PLEASE GIVE ME WISDOM AND COURAGE ABOUT BAPTISM. I WANT TO OBEY YOU AND SHOW OTHERS HOW MUCH I LOVE YOU AND WANT TO FOLLOW YOU! AMEN.

GO TO CHURCH!

Let us go right into the presence of God with sincere hearts fully trusting him. For our guilty consciences have been sprinkled with Christ's blood to make us clean, and our bodies have been washed with pure water. Let us hold tightly without wavering to the hope we affirm, for God can be trusted to keep his promise. Let us think of ways to motivate one another to acts of love and good works. And let us not neglect our meeting together, as some people do, but encourage one another, especially now that the day of his return is drawing near.

HEBREWS 10:22–25 NLT

Going to a good church (one that teaches about the *whole* Bible in context) might not be popular according to the ways of the world, but it's important to love church anyway. The Bible tells us that we need to meet regularly with other Christians who love and trust Jesus as their Savior too and who love continually learning from the whole Word of God.

We need to worship and learn more about God together. And we need to encourage, comfort, and take good care of one another!

HEAVENLY FATHER, THANK YOU FOR ALL THE CHRISTIANS WHO ARE IN MY LIFE AND FOR THE ONES ALL OVER THE WORLD! HELP US TO LOVE GETTING TOGETHER AT CHURCH TO GROW CLOSER TO YOU AND TO ENCOURAGE ONE ANOTHER IN LIFE AND FAITH. AMEN.

MORE ABOUT CHURCH

Those who believed what Peter said were baptized and added to the church that day—about 3,000 in all. All the believers devoted themselves to the apostles' teaching, and to fellowship, and to sharing in meals (including the Lord's Supper), and to prayer.

Acts 2:41–42 NLT

Spend some quiet time today praying for the universal church and for your church. The universal church is everyone all over the world who believes in Jesus as Savior; and if you belong to a local church, you have a group of people who are your church family. You can pray for the universal church and for your local church. You can pray for the protection of everyone in church. You can pray for the pastor, leaders, and volunteers. You can pray for the people who are members and the people who attend. You can pray for churches to carefully preach and follow God's Word and glorify Him in everything. You can pray that God brings more and more people to hear His truth and experience His love at church. You can ask God to show you how you can be an active part of your church.

DEAR GOD, I PRAY FOR THE UNIVERSAL CHURCH, FOR MY CHURCH, AND FOR ALL THOSE WHO NEED TO COME TO CHURCH TO LEARN MORE ABOUT YOU. I ALSO ASK THAT YOU WOULD HELP ME TO SERVE AND BE ACTIVE IN CHURCH ALL MY LIFE. AMEN.

KEEP KNOWING GOD BETTER

I pray that the great God and Father of our Lord Jesus Christ may give you the wisdom of His Spirit. Then you will be able to understand the secrets about Him as you know Him better. . . . I pray that you will know about the hope given by God's call. I pray that you will see how great the things are that He has promised to those who belong to Him. I pray that you will know how great His power is for those who have put their trust in Him. It is the same power that raised Christ from the dead.

EPHESIANS 1:17–20 NLV

In your quiet time today, focus on these things God wants for you:

- To have the wisdom of His Spirit
- To know Him more and more
- To have great hope in Him
- To see what awesome blessings He has promised for all who belong to Him
- To know how much power He has for all who trust in Him—the same great power that raised Jesus from death to life

DEAR GOD, I WANT TO KEEP KNOWING YOU BETTER! I WANT TO KEEP LEARNING MORE ABOUT YOUR PROMISES, YOUR WISDOM, YOUR HOPE, AND YOUR POWER! AMEN.

THE FIRST COMMANDMENT WITH A PROMISE

Children, obey your parents in the Lord, for this is right. "Honor your father and mother"—which is the first commandment with a promise—"so that it may go well with you and that you may enjoy long life on the earth."

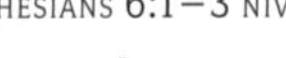

Ephesians 6:1–3 NIV

You're a teen, and right now so many people in the world will give you the idea that it's not cool or popular to obey and respect your parents. These sources will tell you it's more fun to break the good rules you've been given—and even if you get in trouble, at least you'll be getting some attention for it.

But what does God's Word say? It says to honor your father and mother, and that's the first command from God that comes with a promise: "so that it may go well with you and that you may enjoy long life on the earth." Sounds pretty important and worth it, doesn't it?

LORD, EVEN WHEN I DON'T FEEL LIKE IT AND EVEN WHEN I FEEL PRESSURE TO DISOBEY AND DISRESPECT MY PARENTS, HELP ME TO DO MY VERY BEST TO OBEY AND RESPECT AND HONOR AND LOVE THEM WELL. WHEN I DO THOSE THINGS, I'M ALSO OBEYING AND HONORING YOU, AND I TRUST YOU WILL BLESS ME FOR IT—JUST AS YOU'VE PROMISED. AMEN.

WITH GOD THERE IS FORGIVENESS

If you, LORD, kept a record of sins, Lord, who could stand? But with you there is forgiveness, so that we can, with reverence, serve you. I wait for the LORD, my whole being waits, and in his word I put my hope. I wait for the Lord more than watchmen wait for the morning, more than watchmen wait for the morning. Israel, put your hope in the LORD, for with the LORD is unfailing love and with him is full redemption. He himself will redeem Israel from all their sins.

PSALM 130:3–8 NIV

Have you ever felt like you've messed up so badly, made such a big mistake or so many little mistakes that you can never be okay again? If so, don't lose hope. There is still hope and peace for you, because God is the one who forgives. You can run to Him no matter how badly you've messed up. You can admit your sin and let Him cover you with His mercy and grace.

DEAR LORD, I'M SO, SO VERY SORRY. I CAN'T BELIEVE I MESSED UP SO BADLY. I ADMIT WHAT I DID, AND I NEED YOUR HELP. THANK YOU FOR BEING THE ONE WHO FORGIVES. I NEED YOUR GRACE AND MERCY. PLEASE GUIDE ME BACK TO YOUR GOOD PATH. AMEN.

YOU NEED GOD'S WORD, PART 1

All Scripture is God-breathed and is useful for teaching, rebuking, correcting and training in righteousness, so that the servant of God may be thoroughly equipped for every good work.

2 Timothy 3:16–17 NIV

God can communicate with us in any way He chooses. He shows us He is real by His amazing creation all around us. He proves Himself to us when we talk to Him and He answers our prayers. He shows us His love in endless ways and through so many people who take care of us and encourage us and bless us. And He speaks to us in written words, especially through the Bible. We must choose to believe the Bible as God's main way of teaching and guiding us, and then we read it, follow it, and put it into action in our lives.

DEAR GOD, PLEASE HELP ME TO LOVE YOUR WORD AND THE WAY YOU GUIDE ME WITH IT. HELP ME TO WANT TO READ IT EVERY DAY AND LEARN MORE ABOUT YOU AND HOW YOU WANT TO LEAD ME IN THE BEST KIND OF LIFE. AMEN.

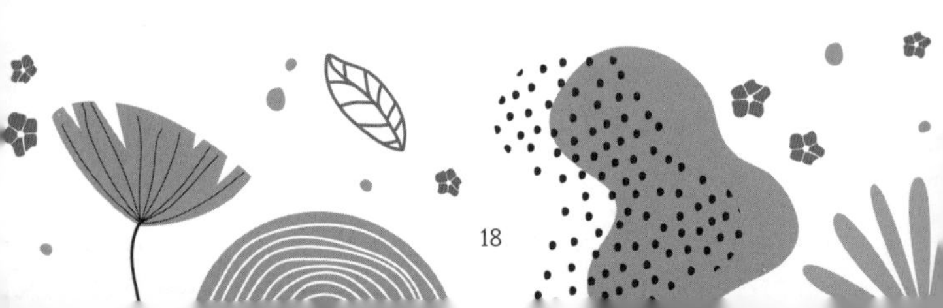

YOU NEED GOD'S WORD, PART 2

For the word of God is alive and active. Sharper than any double-edged sword, it penetrates even to dividing soul and spirit, joints and marrow; it judges the thoughts and attitudes of the heart. Nothing in all creation is hidden from God's sight. Everything is uncovered and laid bare before the eyes of him to whom we must give account.

HEBREWS 4:12–13 NIV

God's Word is not just some ancient book that looks nice sitting on a shelf. It is alive and powerful as we read it. God uses it to speak to us. And "everything that was written in the Holy Writings long ago was written to teach us. By not giving up, God's Word gives us strength and hope" (Romans 15:4 NLV).

PLEASE SPEAK DIRECTLY TO ME THROUGH YOUR WORD EVERY DAY, LORD. TEACH ME AND HELP ME TO LISTEN, LEARN, AND OBEY YOU WELL. AMEN.

YOU NEED GOD'S WORD, PART 3

The grass withers, the flower fades,
but the word of our God will stand forever.

ISAIAH 40:8 ESV

Because the Bible is our main source of wisdom given to us by God, we should make it a regular part of our daily lives. We shouldn't just flip through it occasionally. We shouldn't just carry it to church and leave it to collect dust on the shelf the rest of the week. If we spend time reading God's Word regularly and praying to God as we do, we will learn more and more about Him and His people and how He wants His Word to help us in everything we do.

DEAR GOD, PLEASE HELP ME TO LOVE YOUR WORD AND SPEND TIME READING AND STUDYING IT REGULARLY. HELP ME TO UNDERSTAND IT. I WANT TO HEAR FROM YOU AND GROW IN WISDOM AS I GROW CLOSER TO YOU. AMEN.

FILL YOUR LIFE WITH THE MESSAGE OF CHRIST

Let the message about Christ, in all its richness, fill your lives. Teach and counsel each other with all the wisdom he gives. Sing psalms and hymns and spiritual songs to God with thankful hearts.

Colossians 3:16 NLT

Everything we put into our minds through our eyes and ears affects what we say and do. Colossians 3:16 helps us with this. If we let all the teachings of Jesus fill our lives—meaning we focus on, listen to, and obey them above every other influence in our lives—we will have lives that are rich and full of wisdom. ("Richness" in this case doesn't necessarily mean a life full of lots of money, but it means a life full of all the goodness God wants to give us, especially the things money can never buy.) So, as you make choices about what you put into your mind, you can ask yourself, *Does this help me to focus on God and following Jesus? If not, what could I choose instead that would help me focus on Him?*

DEAR GOD, PLEASE HELP ME TO MAKE EVEN THE SMALLEST CHOICES IN MY LIFE WITH WISDOM FROM YOU. PLEASE HELP ME TO STRIVE TO DO AND SAY ALL THINGS TO BRING HONOR TO YOU. AMEN.

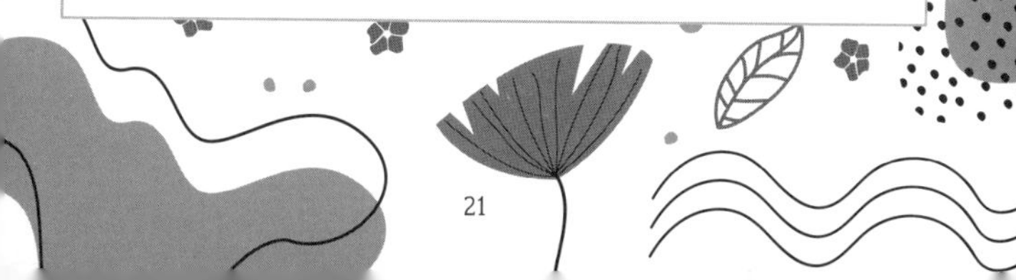

ROCK SOLID

"Anyone who listens to my teaching and follows it is wise, like a person who builds a house on solid rock. Though the rain comes in torrents and the floodwaters rise and the winds beat against that house, it won't collapse because it is built on bedrock. But anyone who hears my teaching and doesn't obey it is foolish, like a person who builds a house on sand. When the rains and floods come and the winds beat against that house, it will collapse with a mighty crash."

MATTHEW 7:24–27 NLT

We could spend quiet time reading the Bible for hours every day, and it wouldn't matter one bit if we didn't learn from it and do what it says. Jesus taught that a person who listens to Him but doesn't obey Him is like a person who builds a house with no solid foundation. When floods come, the house will be destroyed. And when troubles come to people who only hear but don't obey Jesus, they won't be able to stand strong either.

> YOU ARE MY SOLID ROCK, JESUS. I WANT NOT JUST TO HEAR YOU BUT TO OBEY YOU AND STAND STRONG IN YOU NOW AND FOREVER. AMEN.

WHAT TO DO WITH A BROKEN HEART, PART 1

"I have told you these things, so that in me you may have peace. In this world you will have trouble. But take heart! I have overcome the world."

JOHN 16:33 NIV

All kinds of sad things can—and will—happen to us or people we know: loved ones and pets die, parents get divorced, friends betray us. Houses burn down; favorite things get stolen. People get sick or injured. Friends and loved ones move far away, and we miss them. In any of these scenarios, we have a very important choice to make—will we get closer to God or further away? Will we choose to let Him help and comfort us, or will we choose to hold on to anger and blame God?

When life is sad and difficult, the wise choice is to grow closer to God. Psalm 34:17–18 (NLV) says, "Those who are right with the Lord cry, and He hears them. And He takes them from all their troubles. The Lord is near to those who have a broken heart."

WHEN MY HEART FEELS BROKEN, I DON'T WANT TO TURN AWAY FROM YOU, LORD. HELP ME TO CHOOSE TO MOVE CLOSER TO YOU. REMIND ME THAT YOU ARE NEAR AND THAT YOU WANT TO HEAL MY BROKEN HEART. AMEN.

WHAT TO DO WITH A BROKEN HEART, PART 2

[God] heals those who have a broken heart. He heals their sorrows.

Psalm 147:3 NLV

If you have a broken bone, you don't run away screaming from the doctors and nurses who can fix it. That would be stupid! You might feel like doing that on the inside, but it would be so much worse (and more painful) never to fix the broken bone at all. It's like that with a broken heart.

God is the only one who can truly heal broken hearts. Choosing to get closer to Him when you have a broken heart doesn't mean you instantly feel all better. You will still hurt, and you might feel all kinds of emotions, including anger and fear. But if you let Him, God will comfort you and help you with your emotions. It takes time to heal broken hearts, though, just like broken bones take time to heal. So keep praying to God. Keep reading the Bible. Keep going to church and letting other people who love God encourage you too. God will show you His love and care in many ways as He heals you.

DEAR GOD, PLEASE HELP ME TO REMEMBER THAT IT TAKES TIME TO HEAL MY BROKEN HEART. PLEASE COMFORT ME AND SHOW ME YOUR LOVE IN MANY WAYS. AMEN.

SHINE BRIGHT!

"You are the light of the world—like a city on a hilltop that cannot be hidden. No one lights a lamp and then puts it under a basket. Instead, a lamp is placed on a stand, where it gives light to everyone in the house. In the same way, let your good deeds shine out for all to see, so that everyone will praise your heavenly Father."

MATTHEW 5:14–16 NLT

"You are the light of the world." Remind yourself of this truth all the time because there's no better motivation than that!

This is what Jesus has said of us when we trust Him as Savior. And so, with the Holy Spirit in us, our job is to shine our lights so that others will want to trust Jesus as Savior and praise God too! We don't ever want to hide our light. The dark world around us needs the good news and love of Jesus so very much, so let's do good things boldly and courageously to shine as brightly as we can!

DEAR JESUS, THANK YOU FOR CALLING ME THE LIGHT OF THE WORLD. I WANT TO SHINE BRIGHTLY TO EVERYONE AROUND ME TO SHARE YOUR TRUTH AND LOVE—AND GIVE GOD ALL THE PRAISE! AMEN.

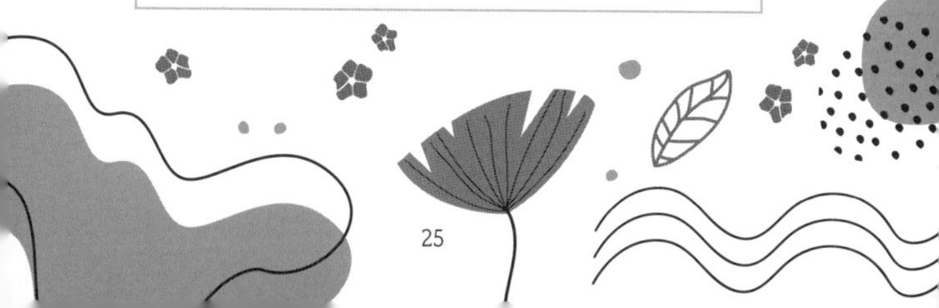

GREAT AND MIGHTY LOVE

Who shall separate us from the love of Christ? Shall trouble or hardship or persecution or famine or nakedness or danger or sword? . . . No, in all these things we are more than conquerors through him who loved us. For I am convinced that neither death nor life, neither angels nor demons, neither the present nor the future, nor any powers, neither height nor depth, nor anything else in all creation, will be able to separate us from the love of God that is in Christ Jesus our Lord.

ROMANS 8:35, 37–39 NIV

What makes you feel down and depressed? Life can be *a lot*. And so, we need regular quiet time with Jesus to rest and get a break and find peace—time to get away from the terrible things going on in our lives and in the world around us. This scripture from Romans reminds us that not even the very worst things of this world can keep us from God's great and mighty love for us through Jesus.

JESUS, THANK YOU THAT ABSOLUTELY NOTHING CAN STOP YOUR INCREDIBLE LOVE FOR ME OR PREVENT ME FROM RECEIVING IT. AMEN.

PERFECT UNITY

Be patient with each other, making allowance for each other's faults because of your love. Make every effort to keep yourselves united in the Spirit, binding yourselves together with peace.

Ephesians 4:2–3 NLT

In your quiet time today, pray for unity among followers of Jesus. We should want to be like-minded and stand strong together, mutually encouraged by our common love of our Savior, Jesus Christ.

Jesus even prayed about unity for all believers: "I am praying not only for these disciples but also for all who will ever believe in me through their message. I pray that they will all be one, just as you and I are one—as you are in me, Father, and I am in you. And may they be in us so that the world will believe you sent me. I have given them the glory you gave me, so they may be one as we are one. I am in them and you are in me. May they experience such perfect unity that the world will know that you sent me and that you love them as much as you love me" (John 17:20–23 NLT).

DEAR JESUS, PLEASE HELP ME TO DO MY PART TO ENCOURAGE OTHERS AND KEEP UNITY WITH THOSE WHO LOVE AND FOLLOW YOU. AMEN.

FIGURING OUT IDENTITY

And God made man in His own likeness. In the likeness of God He made him. He made both male and female.

GENESIS 1:27 NLV

You'll hear all kinds of talk about people trying to figure out their identity these days. But the truth? If we look to God, *that's* where we find our true identity. Genesis 1 makes clear that God made us in His likeness. He made two kinds of people—male and female, who are *equally valuable but different* in body type, strengths, and abilities. Each person also has infinite potential for personality type.

God has given us the Bible to guide us in how to live and love like He does. Galatians 2:20 (NLV) says, "Christ lives in me. The life I now live in this body, I live by putting my trust in the Son of God. He was the One Who loved me and gave Himself for me." And 1 Peter 2:9 (NLV) says, "You are a chosen group of people. . . . You belong to God. He has done this for you so you can tell others how God has called you out of darkness into His great light."

ALMIGHTY GOD, REMIND ME EVERY DAY THAT MY IDENTITY IS FOUND IN YOU. AMEN.

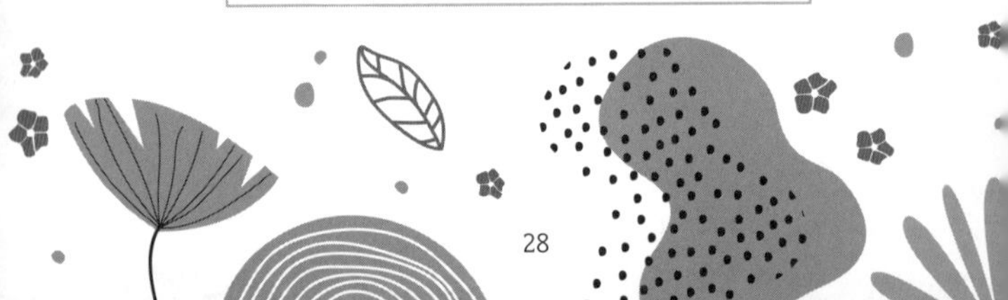

GOOD SHEPHERD

The Lord *is my shepherd; I have all that I need.*
He lets me rest in green meadows; he leads me beside peaceful streams. He renews my strength. He guides me along right paths, bringing honor to his name. Even when I walk through the darkest valley, I will not be afraid, for you are close beside me. Your rod and your staff protect and comfort me. You prepare a feast for me in the presence of my enemies. You honor me by anointing my head with oil. My cup overflows with blessings. Surely your goodness and unfailing love will pursue me all the days of my life, and I will live in the house of the Lord *forever.*

Psalm 23 NLT

Spend some quiet time today focusing on Psalm 23 and thanking and praising God for His love, care, and protection. You can be thankful and at peace because you have the good shepherd watching over you.

DEAR LORD, MY GOOD SHEPHERD, I'D BE SO LOST WITHOUT YOU! THANK YOU FOR ALWAYS GUIDING AND PROTECTING ME. AMEN.

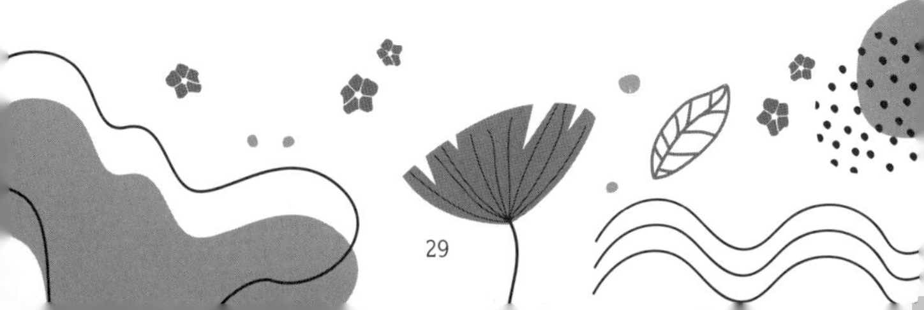

JESUS TAUGHT US HOW TO PRAY

"This, then, is how you should pray: 'Our Father in heaven, hallowed be your name, your kingdom come, your will be done, on earth as it is in heaven. Give us today our daily bread. And forgive us our debts, as we also have forgiven our debtors. And lead us not into temptation, but deliver us from the evil one.'"

MATTHEW 6:9–13 NIV

In your quiet time, focus on how Jesus taught us to pray. He gave us a specific example here in the book of Matthew. In our prayers, we should praise God for who He is and for His awesome holiness. We should ask for His kingdom to come and His will to be done. We should ask Him to meet our needs day by day. We should ask for forgiveness of our sins as we forgive those who sin against us. And we should ask for protection against sin and the evil one.

THANK YOU FOR TEACHING US HOW TO PRAY, JESUS. HELP ME TO REMEMBER AND TO LEARN FROM YOUR PERFECT EXAMPLE. AMEN.

BOLDLY TO THE THRONE

So then, since we have a great High Priest who has entered heaven, Jesus the Son of God, let us hold firmly to what we believe. This High Priest of ours understands our weaknesses, for he faced all of the same testings we do, yet he did not sin. So let us come boldly to the throne of our gracious God. There we will receive his mercy, and we will find grace to help us when we need it most.

HEBREWS 4:14–16 NLT

Talking to well-known people and important leaders can be intimidating. So it's really cool that God's Word tells us that Jesus made the way for us to go to God, who is the King of kings, with total trust and confidence. We can go boldly to His throne! We can even call Him *Abba* (Romans 8:15), which is a term like "Daddy"—that's how much of a close relationship we can have with the one true almighty Creator God, who is Lord of all.

HEAVENLY FATHER, MY ABBA, I'M AMAZED BY YOUR POWER AND MIGHT AS THE KING OF ALL KINGS. YET YOU LOVE ME AND ALLOW ME TO COME BOLDLY TO YOUR THRONE AND EVEN TO CALL YOU DADDY. THANK YOU! AMEN.

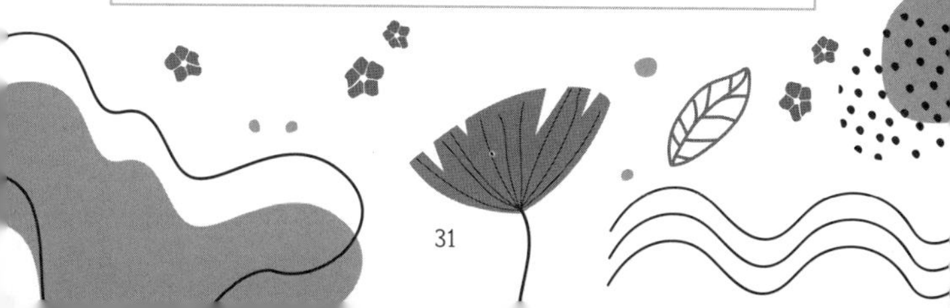

QUIET TIME ANYTIME

I ask for your help, Lord God, and you will keep me safe. Morning, noon, and night you hear my concerns and my complaints. I am attacked from all sides, but you will rescue me unharmed by the battle. You have always ruled, and you will hear me.

Psalm 55:16–19 CEV

It's good to have a set daily quiet time with God to read the Bible and pray. But that doesn't have to be the only time we talk to God throughout the day. This psalm reminds us that morning, noon, and night, God hears any and all of our prayers. He's ready to listen at every moment in between too, plus all night long. If we wake up from a nightmare or a storm or a strange noise, the very first thing we can do is cry out to God in prayer for help and comfort. Isn't it amazing that every single person in the world can pray like this at any time too? He can hear every prayer from every person on earth. That's amazing!

FATHER GOD, THANK YOU FOR BEING AVAILABLE EVERY MOMENT OF EVERY DAY TO HEAR MY PRAYERS AND SPEND TIME WITH ME! AMEN.

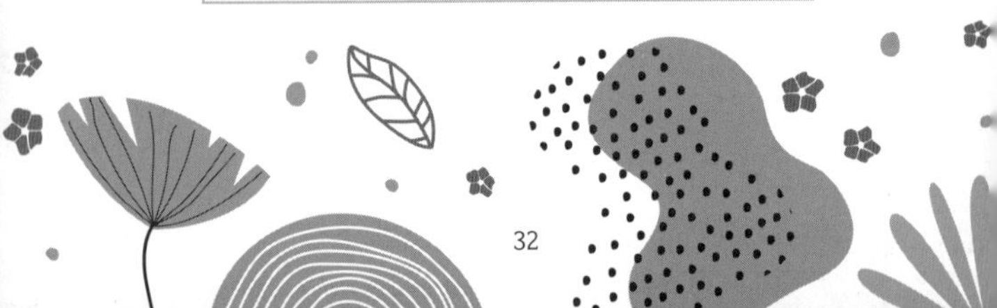

WHAT IS LOVE? PART 1

If I have a faith that can move mountains, but do not have love, I am nothing. . . . These three remain: faith, hope and love. But the greatest of these is love.

1 Corinthians 13:2, 13 NIV

"Love is love." You hear that phrase a lot these days, don't you? But what does it really mean? *Why* do we love? *Who* should we love? Does it matter *how* we love? If everyone has their own idea of love, is anyone right or wrong about love? And if there's no right or wrong kind of love, then wouldn't that make for a lot of confusing chaos?

If you really *think*, it only makes sense that there must be one source where love came from *first* to tell us what true love means. And that first source of love is God. First John 4:16 says, "God is love," and we can learn about real, true love from His Word, the Bible.

DEAR GOD, I NEED YOUR HELP THINKING ABOUT ALL THE DIFFERENT THINGS THE WORLD TELLS ME ABOUT WHAT LOVE IS. PLEASE GUIDE ME WITH YOUR WORD AND YOUR WISDOM AND YOUR TRUTH ABOUT REAL LOVE. AMEN.

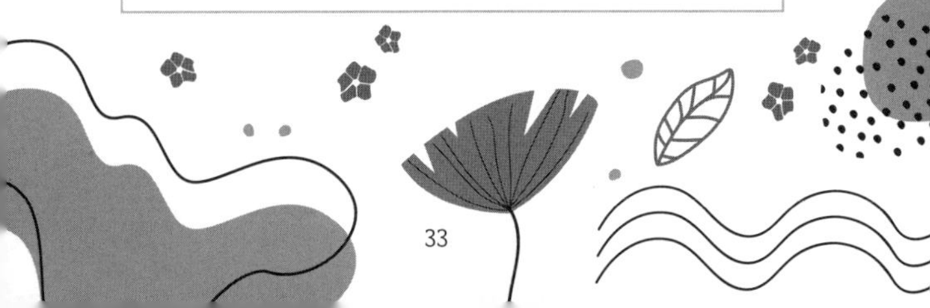

WHAT IS LOVE? PART 2

Dear friends, let us love each other, because love comes from God. Those who love are God's children and they know God. Those who do not love do not know God because God is love. God has shown His love to us by sending His only Son into the world.

1 JOHN 4:7–9 NLV

As you learn more about God and His love by spending quiet time with Him, you'll be filled up and even overflowing with His love! And then with all that extra, you can give it to everyone around you. It's the best way to live—keep spending time with God, get encouraged by His love, share His love with others, and then do that on repeat. What a cool cycle of receiving and giving God's love!

DEAR GOD, REMIND ME EVERY DAY OF WHO I AM—YOUR CHILD. I KNOW YOU ARE REAL LOVE, AND I WANT TO KNOW YOU MORE. PLEASE HELP ME TO SHOW LOVE TO OTHERS IN WAYS THAT ARE JUST LIKE YOUR GREAT LOVE.

WHAT IS LOVE? PART 3

Love does not give up. Love is kind. Love is not jealous. Love does not put itself up as being important. Love has no pride. Love does not do the wrong thing. Love never thinks of itself. Love does not get angry. Love does not remember the suffering that comes from being hurt by someone. Love is not happy with sin. Love is happy with the truth. Love takes everything that comes without giving up. Love believes all things. Love hopes for all things. Love keeps on in all things. Love never comes to an end.

1 Corinthians 13:4–8 NLV

Spend some quiet time today focusing on these scripture verses from 1 Corinthians. As you do, ask God to help you learn and understand more every day about His perfect, true love. Ask Him to help you take all the popular, worldly ideas about love and then compare them to the truth of His Word about what real love is.

DEAR GOD, I BELIEVE YOU ARE LOVE AND THAT EVERYTHING YOU SAY ABOUT LOVE IS REAL AND TRUE. HELP ME TO KEEP LEARNING AND GROWING IN YOUR LOVE. HELP ME TO REJECT EVERY IDEA ABOUT LOVE THE WORLD TELLS ME AND INSTEAD TO FAVOR YOUR LOVE—THE VERY BEST KIND OF LOVE. AMEN.

CONFESS YOUR SINS

If we claim to be without sin, we deceive ourselves and the truth is not in us. If we confess our sins, [God] is faithful and just and will forgive us our sins and purify us from all unrighteousness.

1 John 1:8–9 NIV

Have you ever messed up and hurt a friend's feelings and then wanted to avoid her completely because you felt so guilty? We've all been there. We sometimes want to avoid talking to someone we've hurt because we don't want to admit our mistakes.

We do this same kind of thing to God sometimes. We avoid quiet time with Him because we don't want to admit the ways we are disobeying Him. But that's kind of stupid because He's so full of love and forgiveness for us. He simply wants us to admit our bad choices and turn away from them and turn back to Him. The good rules and guidelines He gives us to obey are because He wants us to have the very best kind of life and rewards, both now and forever.

DEAR GOD, I ADMIT MY BAD CHOICES AND SINS, AND I NEED YOUR HELP TO TURN COMPLETELY AWAY FROM THEM. THANK YOU FOR YOUR LOVE, GRACE, AND FORGIVENESS. AMEN.

CRAVE IT

How can a young person stay pure? By obeying your word. I have tried hard to find you—don't let me wander from your commands. I have hidden your word in my heart, that I might not sin against you. I praise you, O LORD; teach me your decrees. I have recited aloud all the regulations you have given us. I have rejoiced in your laws as much as in riches. I will study your commandments and reflect on your ways. I will delight in your decrees and not forget your word.

PSALM 119:9–16 NLT

The pressures and temptations of this world will try to distract us from spending quiet time with God and learning from the Bible, but we are supposed to love and long for God's Word. More than anything else, we should crave quiet time with God and desire to learn from Him. We need to ask daily for God's help to be able to make this scripture from Psalm 119 true for us today and in the future.

DEAR GOD, I WANT TO LOVE AND CRAVE TIME WITH YOU AND LEARNING FROM YOUR WORD. HELP ME TO HIDE YOUR WORD IN MY HEART AND MIND BY READING IT, LISTENING TO IT, MEMORIZING IT, AND LIVING MY LIFE BY IT. AMEN.

TRUTH MATTERS, PART 1

So stop telling lies. Let us tell our neighbors the truth, for we are all parts of the same body.

Ephesians 4:25 NLT

Telling the truth is a big deal. Proverbs 12:22 (NLV) says, "The Lord hates lying lips, but those who speak the truth are His joy." Since God hates lying lips, it's clearly not okay to lie. And that means we should tell the truth about everything—big things and little things.

Luke 16:10–12 (NLT) says, "If you are faithful in little things, you will be faithful in large ones. But if you are dishonest in little things, you won't be honest with greater responsibilities. And if you are untrustworthy about worldly wealth, who will trust you with the true riches of heaven? And if you are not faithful with other people's things, why should you be trusted with things of your own?"

When we tell the truth, people can trust us, and God will bless us. He will be full of joy because of us.

LORD, PLEASE HELP ME NOT TO LIE—NOT EVEN ABOUT LITTLE THINGS. I WANT TO TELL THE TRUTH AND BE TRUSTWORTHY ALL MY LIFE. AMEN.

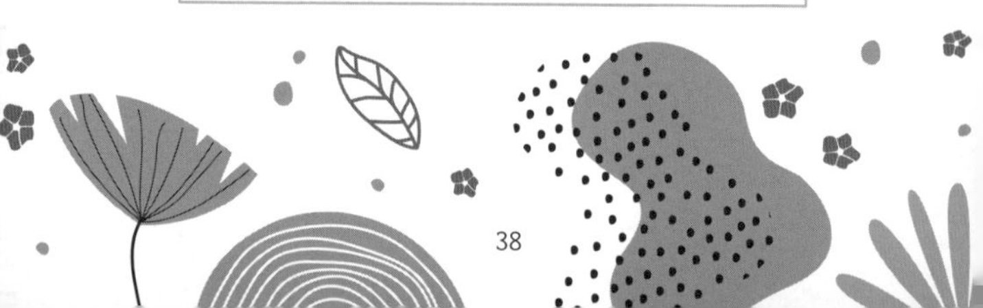

TRUTH MATTERS, PART 2

Show me Your ways, O Lord. Teach me Your paths. Lead me in Your truth and teach me. For You are the God Who saves me.

PSALM 25:4–5 NLV

Honesty and truth are vital, especially in a world where they often seem harder and harder to find. If anyone can have their "own truth" these days, then how can anything be true? What if one person's truth calls another person's truth a lie? What person can say who is right and who is wrong? It's chaos that way!

So let God and the Bible be your number one source of truth, and let these scriptures keep you focused on how important it is!

- "The honor of good people will lead them, but those who hurt others will be destroyed by their own false ways" (Proverbs 11:3 NLV).
- "A false witness will not go unpunished, and a liar will be destroyed" (Proverbs 19:9 NLT).
- "Work hard so you can present yourself to God and receive his approval. Be a good worker, one who does not need to be ashamed and who correctly explains the word of truth" (2 Timothy 2:15 NLT).

DEAR GOD, YOU AND YOUR WORD ARE THE ULTIMATE TRUTH! HELP ME TO LOVE YOU AND THE BIBLE WITH ALL MY HEART. AMEN.

FOLLOW THE LORD'S PATHS

Do not forget my teaching, but keep my commands in your heart, for they will prolong your life many years and bring you peace and prosperity. . . . Trust in the Lord *with all your heart and lean not on your own understanding; in all your ways submit to him, and he will make your paths straight.*

Proverbs 3:1–2, 5–6 niv

Even though it's popular to say, "Follow your heart," it's terrible advice. Before any of us do follow our own hearts, we need to make sure our hearts match up with God's. Too often our own hearts and desires are tempted by sin and everything that's bad for us.

So, God's Word tells us to trust Him with all our hearts and *don't* lean on our own understanding. We need to stay close to Him through reading His Word, praying, worshiping Him, and serving Him. And we constantly need to ask Him to help us submit to Him and His will for us—that's the *only way* we stay on His good, straight path.

DEAR GOD, I WANT TO TRUST IN YOU MORE THAN MYSELF. PLEASE HELP ME TO FOLLOW MY HEART *ONLY* WHEN IT'S MATCHING UP WITH YOURS BECAUSE I'M SUBMITTED TO YOU AND YOUR WILL. AMEN.

LAUGH A LOT

We were filled with laughter, and we sang for joy. And the other nations said, "What amazing things the Lord has done for them." Yes, the Lord has done amazing things for us! What joy!

Psalm 126:2–3 NLT

Aren't you glad God gave us the gift of laughter? It's so good for us to be happy and joyful! Proverbs 17:22 (ESV) says, "A joyful heart is good medicine, but a crushed spirit dries up the bones."

Think about your favorite people to laugh with. Spend some quiet time today thanking God for their part in your life and the joy they bring to you. Ask God to help you grow closer to Him—the source of all authentic joy!

DEAR GOD, I LOVE TO LAUGH AND HAVE FUN, ESPECIALLY WITH FAMILY AND FRIENDS. THANK YOU FOR MY FAVORITE PEOPLE WITH WHOM I SHARE SO MUCH JOY. PLEASE HELP US TO GROW CLOSER TO YOU, FOR YOU ARE THE GIVER OF ALL REAL JOY—JOY THAT WILL LAST FOREVER. AMEN.

EVEN FROM WITHIN YOUR MOTHER'S WOMB

You formed me in my mother's womb. I thank you, High God—you're breathtaking! Body and soul, I am marvelously made! . . . You know me inside and out. . . . All the stages of my life were spread out before you, the days of my life all prepared before I'd even lived one day.

Psalm 139:13–16 MSG

From the moment your life began inside your mother's womb, God has been making perfect plans for you. He created every detail about you and knows and loves you with the greatest love. And He made you with free will. You get to choose whether you will love Him back and follow Him or not.

You know it's not real to force someone to be your friend. And God doesn't force anyone to love and follow Him either. He wants you to love and follow Him with real love that you choose. And when you do, He wants to bless you with the very best kind of life—the life He designed you for.

DEAR GOD, I'M GRATEFUL FOR YOUR LOVE. I WANT TO TRULY LOVE YOU IN RETURN AND OBEY YOU EVERY DAY OF MY LIFE. WHEN I MAKE MISTAKES, PLEASE HELP ME TO GET BACK QUICKLY TO FOLLOWING YOU. AMEN.

PRAY FOR HEALING

The people immediately recognized [Jesus] and ran about the whole region and began to bring the sick people on their beds to wherever they heard he was. And wherever he came, in villages, cities, or countryside, they laid the sick in the marketplaces and implored him that they might touch even the fringe of his garment. And as many as touched it were made well.

MARK 6:54–56 ESV

Spend your quiet time today praying for those who are sick and in need of healing. Jesus had power to heal people back in Bible times, and He still has that power today. Sometimes He doesn't heal people here on earth, but we must remember that forever healing is promised in heaven for all who trust in Jesus as the one and only Savior of their sins. There will be no more sickness and dying in heaven (Revelation 21:4). Above all, we should pray for everyone we know to believe in Jesus and have forever life too.

DEAR JESUS, I PRAY FOR YOU TO HEAL SICKNESS AND PAIN HERE ON EARTH, AND MOST OF ALL I PRAY FOR YOU TO HEAL PEOPLE'S HEARTS FOREVER BY HELPING THEM TO TURN TO YOU AS THE ONLY SAVIOR FROM THEIR SINS. AMEN.

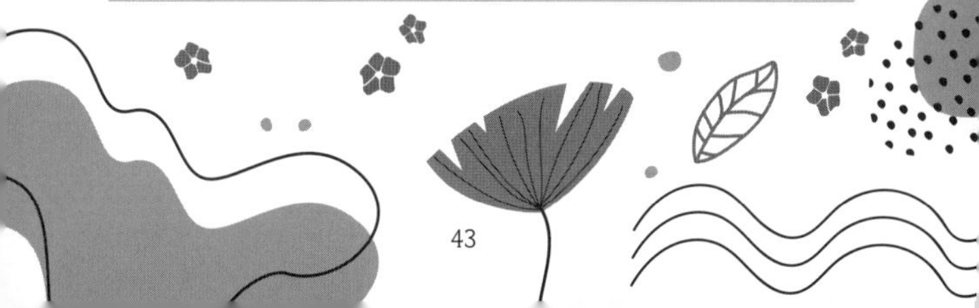

AVOID SINFUL THINGS

I will set no sinful thing in front of my eyes. I hate the work of those who are not faithful. It will not get hold of me. A sinful heart will be far from me. I will have nothing to do with sin.

Psalm 101:3–4 NLV

The writer of this psalm makes a big promise—not to look at any sinful thing. It was probably easier to make that promise back in his time because there were no movies, television series, smartphones, TikTok and YouTube videos, or social media we have vying for our attention today. Therefore, we must be extra careful about what we look at, because the world is overflowing with sinful things that are at our fingertips—and our enemy the devil wants to push those things on us so that we will disobey God and walk away from Him.

DEAR GOD, I WANT TO MAKE THIS PROMISE—I DON'T WANT TO LOOK AT OR WATCH ANYTHING THAT IS SINFUL. I WANT TO KEEP MY MIND AND HEART CLEAN AND FAR AWAY FROM SIN. PLEASE HELP ME. AMEN.

WHEN YOU DON'T KNOW HOW TO PRAY

The Holy Spirit helps us in our weakness. For example, we don't know what God wants us to pray for. But the Holy Spirit prays for us with groanings that cannot be expressed in words. And the Father who knows all hearts knows what the Spirit is saying, for the Spirit pleads for us believers in harmony with God's own will.

ROMANS 8:26–27 NLT

You might sometimes try to spend quiet time with God but sit and think, *I don't know how to pray today*. That's totally okay! Just tell God that. Talk to Him and remember that the Bible tells us that the Holy Spirit helps us when we are weak, and the Holy Spirit prays for us. God knows our hearts. He knows our troubles. He knows what we need. He just wants us to come to Him for help and hope, even when we don't have the words.

DEAR GOD, I COME TO YOU TODAY TO SPEND TIME WITH YOU, BUT I DON'T KNOW WHAT TO SAY. I'M HERE, THOUGH, AND I BELIEVE YOU LOVE ME, AND I BELIEVE THE HOLY SPIRIT IS HERE TO HELP ME. YOU KNOW MY HEART AND THOUGHTS AND EVERYTHING I'M GOING THROUGH. THAT'S A RELIEF AND COMFORT, AND I'M GRATEFUL. AMEN.

ORGANIZE YOUR QUIET TIME

We always pray for you, and we give thanks to God, the Father of our Lord Jesus Christ.

COLOSSIANS 1:3 NLT

If you like to be organized (or need to get better at it), you can organize prayer topics for your quiet time. With either art supplies or a computer program, design a calendar. Once you have it ready, fill it up with specific names of people to pray for and topics and concerns in the world: family members, friends, neighbors, teachers, instructors, coaches, pastors and church leaders and volunteers, police and military, missionaries, health care providers—the list goes on and on! You might be surprised how quickly you fill it up. And of course you can list names and topics more than once. The point is, find creative ways to remember to pray for the specific people and concerns in your life. You can never pray too much!

DEAR GOD, HELP ME TO GET ORGANIZED AND TO REMEMBER SPECIFIC PEOPLE AND REQUESTS IN PRAYER. THANK YOU FOR CARING ABOUT EVERYONE AND EVERYTHING GOING ON IN OUR WORLD AND OUR LIVES. AMEN.

DON'T TRY TO SHOW OFF

"When you pray, don't be like the hypocrites who love to pray publicly on street corners and in the synagogues where everyone can see them. I tell you the truth, that is all the reward they will ever get."

MATTHEW 6:5 NLT

You've probably encountered show-offs in your life—people who try to keep all the attention on themselves. Jesus talked about the kinds of people who even use prayer to show off. And He said not to be like them. Our prayers and quiet time should be a sincere conversation with our heavenly Father, a time of praising Him and asking for His help and learning from Him.

Does this scripture passage from Matthew mean that every single prayer should be said in secret when we're alone? No. However, it is making the point that prayer should be sincere and only to the one true God. And in every prayer, we should place all our attention on God and His power alone, not on ourselves.

DEAR GOD, HELP ME TO HUMBLE MYSELF AND TO PUT ALL ATTENTION ON YOU IN PRAYER AND PRAISE SO THAT OTHERS WILL LOVE AND FOLLOW YOU TOO. AMEN.

TESTS AND TEMPTATION

God blesses those who patiently endure testing and temptation. Afterward they will receive the crown of life that God has promised to those who love him.

James 1:12 NLT

Anyone who thinks that becoming a Christian means an easy life is obviously not reading the Bible or growing closer to God. His Word clearly says that we will be tested, and we will be tempted to do wrong. Even so, it's the best kind of life to love God and trust in and follow Jesus as Lord and Savior.

In every test and temptation, every bit of suffering and heartache, God is working out His good plans in our lives when we faithfully obey Him despite our circumstances. He will continue to bless us with His supernatural comfort and peace and joy even during the trials and pain, until one day we will have complete comfort, peace, and joy—no tears or hardship ever again—when we are at home forever in heaven.

HEAVENLY FATHER, PLEASE HELP ME TO PATIENTLY ENDURE THE TESTING AND TEMPTING IN MY LIFE. I WANT TO PREVAIL OVER THEM BECAUSE I FOLLOW YOU AND BELIEVE IN YOUR ETERNAL BLESSINGS.

GOD IS ALWAYS THERE, EVERYWHERE

Where can I go from your Spirit? Where can I flee from your presence? If I go up to the heavens, you are there; if I make my bed in the depths, you are there. If I rise on the wings of the dawn, if I settle on the far side of the sea, even there your hand will guide me, your right hand will hold me fast.

Psalm 139:7–10 NIV

There is no place on earth where you are ever away—or hidden—from God. Through His Spirit, He is with you every moment, no matter where you go or what you do. God sees and knows everything—He even knows your every thought! This might seem scary at first, but it shouldn't bother you. Instead, it should make you feel loved and cared for. God wants to help guide and protect you anytime and anywhere.

DEAR GOD, THANK YOU FOR BEING MY CONSTANT COMPANION. YOU ARE ALWAYS THERE, EVERYWHERE! I'M NEVER ALONE AND HAVE NOTHING TO FEAR WITH YOU RIGHT BESIDE ME! AMEN.

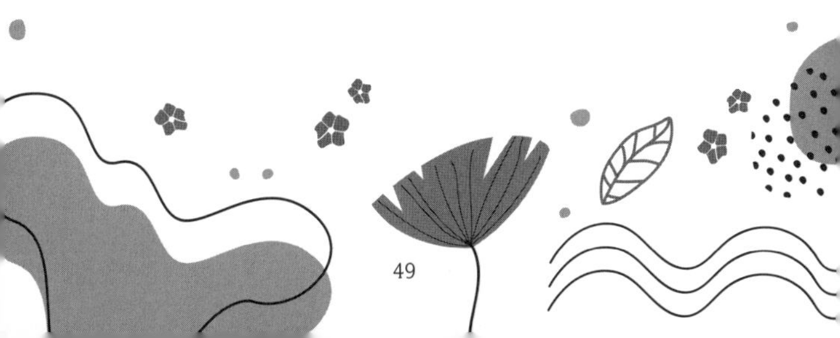

DON'T HOLD ON TO SIN

Come and hear, all who fear God, and I will tell you what He has done for me. I cried to Him with my mouth and praised Him with my tongue. The Lord will not hear me if I hold on to sin in my heart. But it is sure that God has heard. He has listened to the voice of my prayer. Honor and thanks be to God! He has not turned away from my prayer or held His loving-kindness from me.

Psalm 66:16–20 NLV

When we pray, do we want God to ignore us? Of course not! So, if we want Him to listen and answer in His perfect timing, we must regularly admit to Him when we sin. He knows our sins anyway because He sees and knows everything. But we have to *confess* our sins to Him.

The Bible is clear that God forgives us and removes our sins as far as the east is from the west (Psalm 103:12), but we can't hold on to sins. We need to admit them, ask forgiveness from them, let them go, and run far away from them with God's help.

DEAR GOD, I MAKE A LOT OF MISTAKES, BUT I DON'T WANT TO HIDE THEM OR PRETEND LIKE I'M PERFECT—BECAUSE I'M SURELY NOT! I CONFESS THESE SINS RIGHT NOW: ________________. PLEASE FORGIVE ME. THANK YOU, FATHER! AMEN.

BE HUMBLE AND LIFTED UP

Humble yourselves before the Lord,
and he will lift you up in honor.
James 4:10 NLT

In your quiet time today, think about what it means to be humble. It's the opposite of being proud and thinking too highly of yourself. It's good to be confident and have good self-esteem, but it's not good to take that so far that you brag and think you are better than others, that you can never make a mistake, that you never need to apologize to others, or that you have no need for God in your life. Being humble means that you know you mess up sometimes and need forgiveness and grace from God and from others. It also means that you know there are always ways you can learn and grow.

DEAR GOD, PLEASE HELP ME TO KNOW THE DIFFERENCE BETWEEN BEING PROUD AND BEING HUMBLE. HELP ME TO BE HUMBLE AND ALWAYS AWARE OF HOW MUCH I NEED YOUR GRACE AND LOVE!

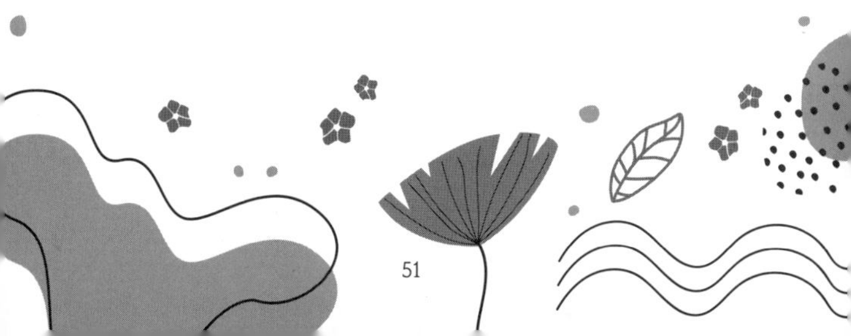

WHAT'S KEEPING YOU FROM GOD'S GOOD PLANS?

Let us strip off every weight that slows us down, especially the sin that so easily trips us up. And let us run with endurance the race God has set before us. We do this by keeping our eyes on Jesus, the champion who initiates and perfects our faith. Because of the joy awaiting him, he endured the cross, disregarding its shame. Now he is seated in the place of honor beside God's throne.

HEBREWS 12:1–2 NLT

What things in your life are keeping you from doing what you should? Maybe it's too much time on your phone. Maybe it's being too focused on sports and activities and not focused enough on time with God and with loved ones and on homework and responsibilities. God has good plans for all of us, but we must look to Jesus and get rid of the stuff that keeps us away from those plans.

DEAR GOD, I WANT TO BE ON THE PATH THAT YOU HAVE SET OUT FOR ME. PLEASE HELP ME TO GET RID OF ANYTHING IN MY LIFE THAT IS KEEPING ME FROM YOUR GOOD PLANS. AMEN.

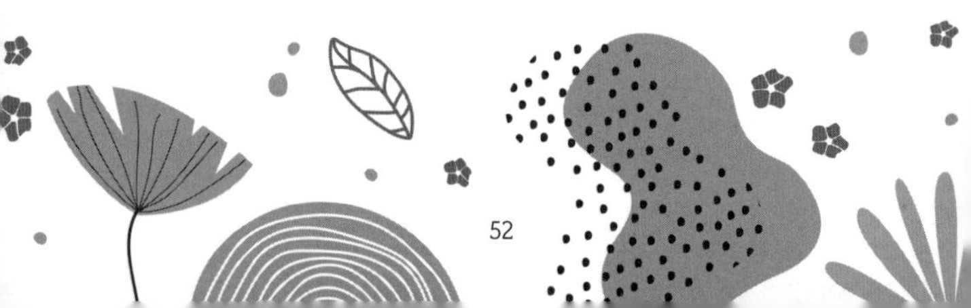

HOW TO HANDLE ANGER

"In your anger do not sin": Do not let the sun go down while you are still angry, and do not give the devil a foothold.

EPHESIANS 4:26–27 NIV

Everyone gets angry sometimes, and the Bible doesn't say anger is always bad. God knows we will and should be angry sometimes. But the Bible does say not to sin when we are angry. We shouldn't let anger control us. That's extremely difficult sometimes.

So, the moment we feel anger start to rise inside, we need to train ourselves to take deep breaths and slow down—then pray and ask God how we should react. His Word says in Proverbs 14:29 (NLV), "He who is slow to get angry has great understanding, but he who has a quick temper makes his foolish way look right." And James 1:19 (NLV) says, "Everyone should listen much and speak little. He should be slow to become angry."

PLEASE HELP ME SLOW DOWN WHEN I START TO FEEL ANGRY, LORD. HELP ME TO STOP AND ASK YOU HOW TO HANDLE MY ANGER. I DON'T WANT TO SIN WHEN I AM ANGRY. INSTEAD, I WANT TO DEAL WITH IT IN WAYS THAT HONOR YOU AND SHARE YOUR TRUTH AND LOVE. AMEN.

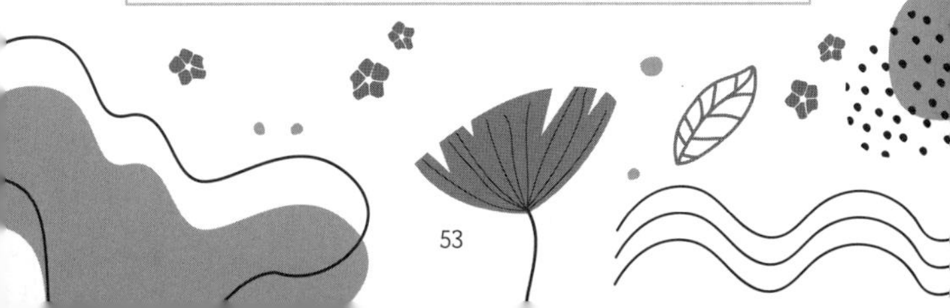

THOSE EMBARRASSING MOMENTS

The Lord will be your confidence.

Proverbs 3:26 ESV

We've all done things that are embarrassing and awkward—those ridiculous things that make us want to melt into a puddle on the floor or become invisible. And, after the moment is over, the weirdness can live on in our minds for a long time. But the awkward or embarrassing moment is usually much bigger in our own minds than in the minds of others. Yes, whoever was watching might remember for a while. You might even get teased a little. But that shows others' character, not yours.

You can choose to show strong character and courage by acknowledging that everyone has embarrassing moments. So shake it off. Hold your head high and remember that you are a child of the one true God who loves you and is always looking out for you—no matter what embarrassing things you (and everyone else) might do.

HEAVENLY FATHER, PLEASE COMFORT ME AND HELP ME TO SHAKE IT OFF WHEN I'M EMBARRASSED AND FEELING AWKWARD. HELP ME TO REMEMBER THAT YOU ARE MY CONFIDENCE. THANK YOU FOR LOVING ME NO MATTER WHAT. AMEN.

IS FRUIT GROWING IN YOUR LIFE?

The Holy Spirit produces this kind of fruit in our lives: love, joy, peace, patience, kindness, goodness, faithfulness, gentleness, and self-control.

GALATIANS 5:22–23 NLT

How do you know if the Holy Spirit is working in your life? One way is that you will see what the Bible calls *the fruit of the Holy Spirit*. These are the things that give you good character and make you more and more like Jesus.

Spend quiet time today thinking about if you are seeing love, joy, peace, patience, kindness, goodness, faithfulness, gentleness, and self-control growing in your life. What specific ways? And how much? Celebrate the ways fruit is already growing, and keep looking to produce more. God is happy to help you with this as you love and obey Him.

HEAVENLY FATHER, I WANT TO SEE EVIDENCE OF YOUR SPIRIT'S WORK IN MY LIFE. PLEASE GROW THE FRUIT OF THE SPIRIT IN MY LIFE. THANK YOU! AMEN.

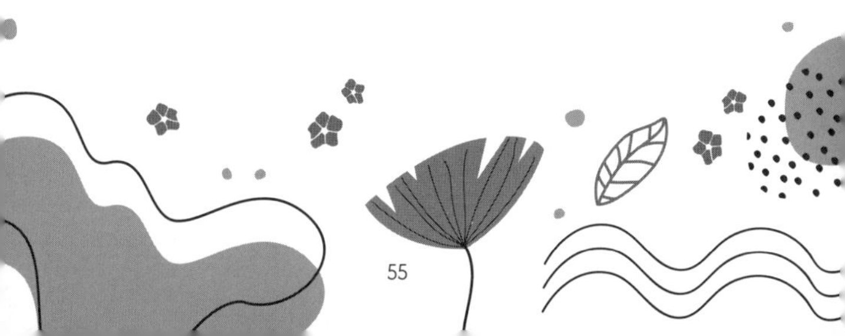

DON'T FEAR THOSE WHO THREATEN YOU

"Don't be afraid of those who threaten you. For the time is coming when everything that is covered will be revealed, and all that is secret will be made known to all."

MATTHEW 10:26 NLT

You never need to be afraid of any threats or bullies or people acting like jerks in your life, for they will be found out—if not right away, then eventually. Bad consequences are coming their way. Trust that above all, God sees and cares and will bring true justice. Keep praying and asking Him to deliver justice quickly, and ask for wisdom on how to stand up to opponents. While you're at it, ask for protection and courage too!

ALMIGHTY GOD, REMIND ME EVERY DAY THAT I DON'T NEED TO BE AFRAID OF ANYONE WHO THREATENS ME. YOU SEE ALL, KNOW ALL, AND WILL MAKE EVERYTHING RIGHT WITH TRUE JUSTICE AND IN YOUR PERFECT TIMING. AMEN.

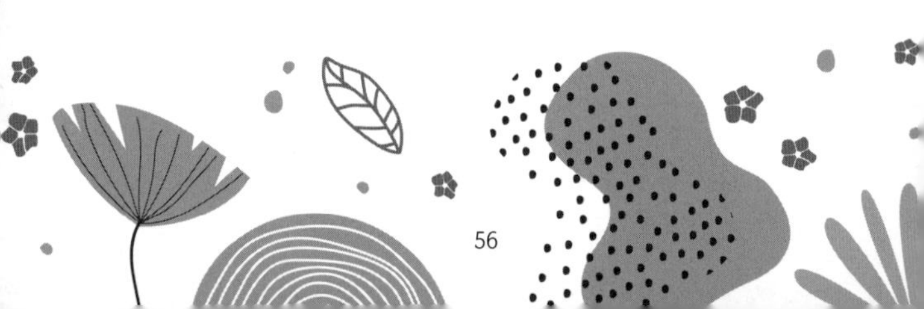

FOLLOW DANIEL'S EXAMPLE

Now when Daniel learned that the decree had been published, he went home to his upstairs room where the windows opened toward Jerusalem. Three times a day he got down on his knees and prayed, giving thanks to his God, just as he had done before.

Daniel 6:10 NIV

In the Bible, Daniel is one of our best examples of being faithful at having regular quiet time. Three times each day he spent time in prayer and giving thanks to God. Even when he knew he might be thrown into a den of lions for praying, he never stopped. And then he *was* thrown into that den.

But, with an astounding miracle, God shut the mouths of the lions so that they didn't harm Daniel. And even more exciting, the next day King Darius was so astonished by this miracle that he chose to believe in God and announced that all the people of his nation should too!

DEAR GOD, HELP ME TO BE FAITHFUL AND BRAVE LIKE DANIEL, WHO NEVER STOPPED PRAYING TO YOU—EVEN WHEN HIS FAITHFULNESS TO YOU PUT HIM IN GREAT DANGER. PLEASE LET ME SEE GREAT MIRACLES HAPPEN WHEN I FOLLOW YOU! AMEN.

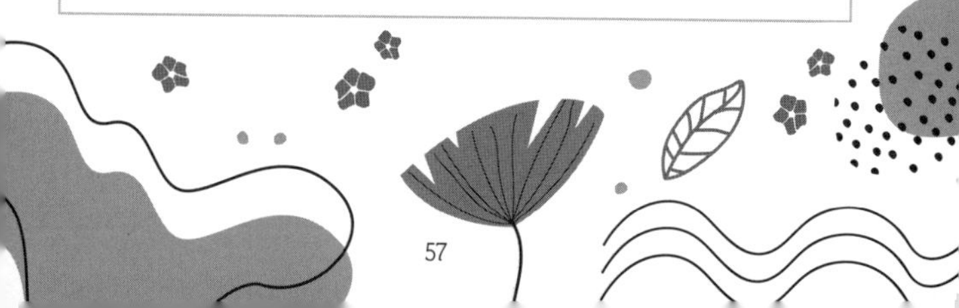

THANK GOD FOR FAMILY AND FRIENDS

A friend is always loyal, and a brother is born to help in time of need.

PROVERBS 17:17 NLT

Who do you talk to or text the most? Do you ever stop to thank God for the people you are closest to? Spend some quiet time today thinking of all the reasons you love them and all the fun experiences you share. Think of all the times and ways you help and support and encourage each other. Thank and praise God for putting them into your life and ask Him to bless and guide them. If they don't trust in Jesus as their Savior, ask God to help you point them to Jesus as the one and only way, truth, and life.

DEAR GOD, THANK YOU FOR MY AWESOME FRIENDS AND FAMILY. PLEASE HELP ME TO LOVE AND ENCOURAGE THEM IN THE WAYS YOU WANT ME TO. HELP OUR RELATIONSHIPS TO GROW IN ALL THE BEST WAYS—AND ESPECIALLY HELP US TO GROW CLOSER TO YOU! AMEN.

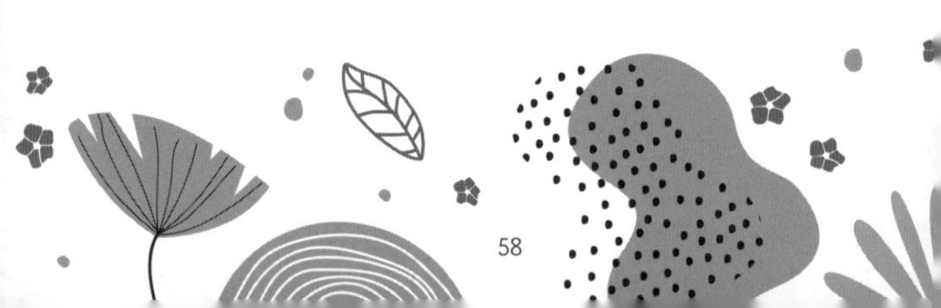

ANGELS?

If you make the Lord your refuge, if you make the Most High your shelter, no evil will conquer you; no plague will come near your home. For he will order his angels to protect you wherever you go. They will hold you up with their hands so you won't even hurt your foot on a stone.

Psalm 91:9–12 NLT

A lot of stories get made up about angels, and many are just fiction. But angels themselves are not just fiction. The Bible says they are real, and they help take care of us and protect us. Isn't that awesome to think about?

Hebrews 1:14 (NLV) says, "Are not all the angels spirits who work for God? They are sent out to help those who are to be saved from the punishment of sin." And you can look up many more verses in the Bible about angels too—and be stronger and braver knowing that God can send them to help you with anything at any time.

ALMIGHTY GOD, IT'S AMAZING TO THINK ABOUT ANGELS AND HOW YOU SEND THEM TO HELP AND RESCUE PEOPLE. YOU ARE AWESOME, AND I LOVE YOU. I'M THANKFUL TO BE YOUR CHILD! AMEN.

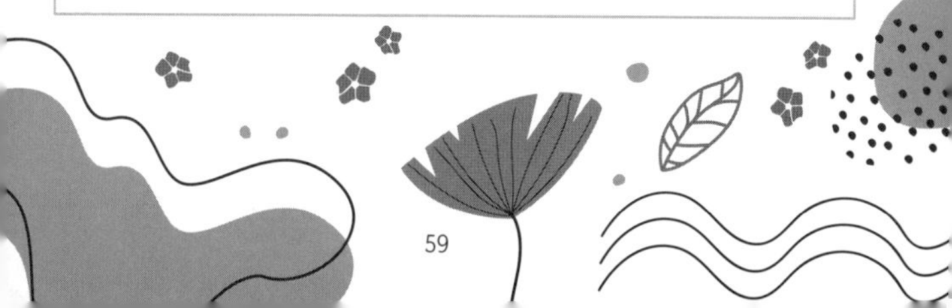

THE BEAUTIFUL WORK OF GOD'S HAND

But now, O Lord, you are our Father; we are the clay, and you are our potter; we are all the work of your hand.

Isaiah 64:8 ESV

Do you remember making an art project when you were really little? You probably knew exactly what it was meant to be, but no one else seemed to. That's because you were the creator, so of course you knew, even if no one else could see it.

Never forget that the one true God is your Creator. Sometimes you might not be sure exactly who you are meant to be and what you're supposed to be doing as you're growing and still figuring out life, but God always knows. Keep following Him and asking Him to guide you into the unique life He made you for and full of the good things He has planned for you.

DEAR GOD, YOU ARE THE POTTER AND I AM THE CLAY. THANK YOU FOR MAKING ME AND HAVING GOOD PLANS FOR ME. PLEASE SHOW ME DAY BY DAY WHAT YOUR GOOD PLANS ARE. I WANT TO FOLLOW YOU FOREVER! AMEN.

FINDING GOOD FRIENDS

Do not be misled: "Bad company corrupts good character."

1 Corinthians 15:33 niv

Spend some time today focusing on prayer for your friends. We all need good friends in our lives, and we need to be good friends to others. But this verse makes it clear that we need to be cautious about friendships too. Bad company and bad friends will corrupt us. We need to know how to figure out if a friend is a good one or not. Your very best friend is Jesus. And the best kind of friends are those who love and follow Him too and who try to be as much like Him as possible. A bad friend will want to lead you into trouble and away from Jesus.

We all need God's help to know which friend is the good kind of friend! So, never stop asking God to show you every friend's true character. He'll show you which friendships to keep and which ones to let go.

I'M SO THANKFUL FOR THE GIFT OF GOOD FRIENDS, LORD. PLEASE GUIDE ME IN FINDING FRIENDSHIPS THAT ARE TRULY GOOD FOR ME, AND HELP ME TO BE CAREFUL WHO I'M FRIENDS WITH, BOTH NOW AND IN THE FUTURE. AMEN.

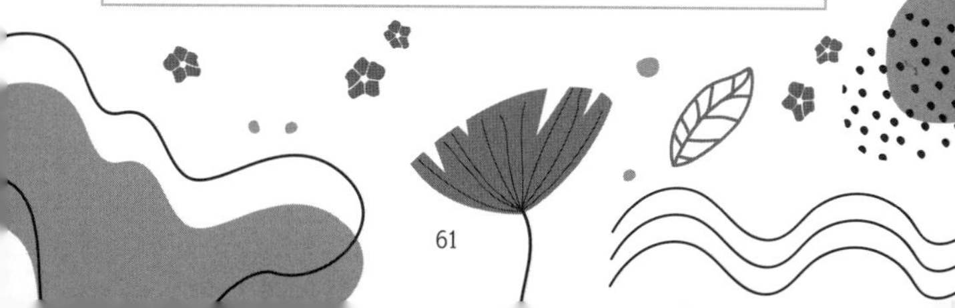

HARD TRUTH

Stay alert! Watch out for your great enemy, the devil. He prowls around like a roaring lion, looking for someone to devour. Stand firm against him, and be strong in your faith. Remember that your family of believers all over the world is going through the same kind of suffering you are.

1 Peter 5:8–9 NLT

This passage in 1 Peter shares the hard truth that those of us who trust in Jesus as Savior have an enemy—the devil—who is like a hungry lion that wants to destroy us in any way possible. We need to know about him and have the courage to fight him.

How can we fight this enemy? By staying close to God. By reading His Word, praying constantly, and being involved in a Bible-teaching church that helps us grow closer to God. By keeping good friendships with people who encourage and support us in our faith. And by being careful to distance ourselves from people who might lead us away from Jesus. The devil wants to destroy us by getting us alone or under bad influences that tempt us to disobey God. But we can always stand up to the enemy and fight with the power God provides!

ALMIGHTY GOD, PLEASE HELP ME TO WATCH OUT FOR THE DEVIL AND TO BE READY TO FIGHT HIM IN YOUR POWER. AMEN.

WE HAVE VICTORY WITH JESUS

"The thief comes only to steal and kill and destroy. I came that they may have life and have it abundantly."

John 10:10 ESV

No matter what the devil tries to do to us, he cannot win. We will always win against our enemy in the end. He might hurt us or make us stumble away from God at times, but he will never defeat us when we trust in Jesus as our Savior.

This passage from the book of John tells us that the devil, who is a robber, wants to steal and destroy every good thing, but Jesus came to give us a great, full life. When Jesus died and then rose again, He showed that absolutely nothing the devil does can ever defeat the powerful love of God and His desire to give us everlasting life with Him.

DEAR GOD, THANK YOU SO MUCH FOR JESUS' RESURRECTION! HE IS PROOF OF YOUR GIFT OF ETERNAL LIFE FOR ME. NOTHING CAN EVER TAKE AWAY THAT MOST VALUABLE GIFT. IT'S AMAZING, AND I'M GRATEFUL! AMEN.

HOW TO LIVE YOUR BEST LIFE

I will give honor and thanks to the Lord, Who has told me what to do. . . . I have placed the Lord always in front of me. Because He is at my right hand, I will not be moved. And so my heart is glad. My soul is full of joy. My body also will rest without fear. For You will not give me over to the grave. And You will not allow Your Holy One to return to dust. You will show me the way of life. Being with You is to be full of joy. In Your right hand there is happiness forever.

Psalm 16:7–11 NLV

God is always with you, and you can live your best life, full of true joy, by keeping Him in front of you—always letting Him lead and doing your best to obey and follow Him.

DEAR LORD OF MY LIFE, I WANT YOU ALWAYS UP FRONT GUIDING ME IN THE WAY I SHOULD GO. I WANT TO FOLLOW YOU AND DO YOUR WILL. THANK YOU FOR NEVER LEAVING ME. IF I EVER WANDER AWAY FROM YOU, PLEASE FORGIVE ME AND HELP ME TO GET BACK ON TRACK QUICKLY. AMEN.

LOOK UP TO THE HEAVENS

"To whom will you compare me? Or who is my equal?" says the Holy One. Lift up your eyes and look to the heavens: Who created all these? He who brings out the starry host one by one and calls forth each of them by name. Because of his great power and mighty strength, not one of them is missing.

Isaiah 40:25–26 NIV

Once in a while, spend some quiet time looking up at the night sky. Think about this passage from Isaiah as you do.

When you focus on how vast the sky is and how our God is so much bigger that He has a name for each of the trillions of stars, you will be astounded! How can anyone help but to be filled with awe! It's amazing that the same almighty God who made the heavens and knows the stars by name made us and knows our names—and takes good care of us too!

ALMIGHTY GOD, I CAN'T EVEN FATHOM HOW BIG AND AWESOME YOU ARE! I AM THANKFUL THAT I CAN TALK TO YOU AND DEPEND ON YOU FOR ANYTHING! AMEN.

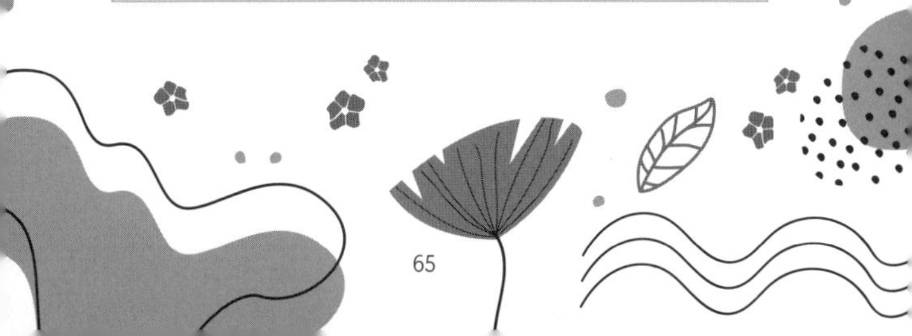

FEELING SAD?

Why am I discouraged? Why is my heart so sad?
I will put my hope in God! I will praise him again—
my Savior and my God! Now I am deeply discouraged,
but I will remember you. . . . Each day the Lord *pours*
his unfailing love upon me, and through each night
I sing his songs, praying to God who gives me life.

Psalm 42:5–6, 8 NLT

Sometimes we just feel sad. Life is full of hard and painful things that make us cry. It's okay to feel the sadness, but eventually we have to take that sadness to God and talk to Him about it. God will help us remember how He has carried us through hard things in the past with His love and kindness, and we can trust that He will do it again and again, whenever we need Him to.

DEAR LORD, WHEN I'M SAD AND WORRIED, PLEASE HELP ME TO PUT MY HOPE BACK IN YOU BECAUSE YOU'VE SHOWN ME HOW YOU WILL ALWAYS CARRY ME THROUGH. AMEN.

INFINITELY MORE

May you experience the love of Christ, though it is too great to understand fully. Then you will be made complete with all the fullness of life and power that comes from God. Now all glory to God, who is able, through his mighty power at work within us, to accomplish infinitely more than we might ask or think. Glory to him in the church and in Christ Jesus through all generations forever and ever! Amen.

EPHESIANS 3:19–21 NLT

God's love is so much bigger and better than anything we can ever even think of or fully comprehend, and He is able to do *infinitely* more than our greatest hopes and dreams! As you pray and ask for His blessings and help in your life, think about how great His love is for you and how His plans for you are always the best. One day we will see exactly how He worked everything together for good for everyone who loves Him (Romans 8:28).

DEAR GOD, THANK YOU FOR YOUR INFINITE, AWESOME LOVE AND POWER! THANK YOU FOR WORKING EVERYTHING TOGETHER FOR GOOD IN MY LIFE. I LOVE YOU! AMEN.

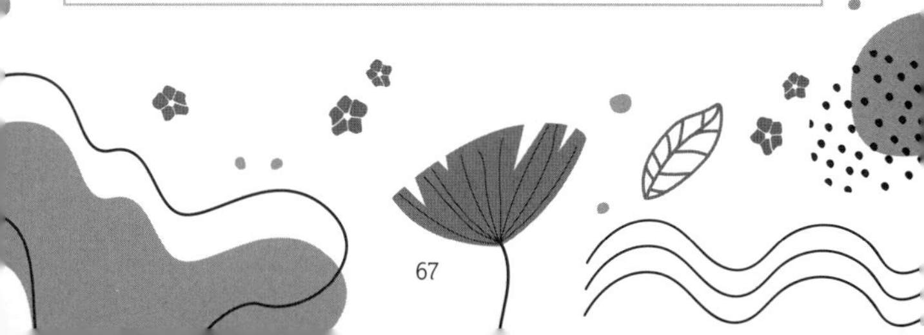

HE WILL LEAD

The Lord went before them by day in a pillar of cloud to lead them along the way, and by night in a pillar of fire to give them light, that they might travel by day and by night. The pillar of cloud by day and the pillar of fire by night did not depart from before the people.

Exodus 13:21–22 ESV

Do you ever wish God would lead you in perfectly clear ways just like He led His people, the Israelites, with the pillars of cloud and fire in the sky when they were wandering in the wilderness? That would be nice, right? Because sometimes we feel like we are wandering in the wilderness too.

We're not always sure where to go and what to do with the problems and troubles and decisions in life. But God knows how to guide us. He might not do it in such dramatic ways as pillars of cloud and fire, but if we keep faith in Him, if we keep asking Him to help, if we keep listening and watching for Him, He will lead us in exactly the ways we need.

DEAR GOD, I NEED YOUR HELP, AND I'M WATCHING FOR YOU. PLEASE GUIDE ME. AMEN.

REST AND WAIT ON THE LORD

Trust in the LORD, and do good; dwell in the land and befriend faithfulness. Delight yourself in the LORD, and he will give you the desires of your heart. Commit your way to the LORD; trust in him, and he will act. He will bring forth your righteousness as the light, and your justice as the noonday. Be still before the LORD and wait patiently for him; fret not yourself over the one who prospers in his way, over the man who carries out evil devices!

PSALM 37:3–7 ESV

In your quiet time today, ask God to help you rest in Him. Ask Him to let you feel all the joy that comes from trusting in Him and doing the good things He wants you to do. He gave you your life, and you can let Him lead it. He wants to bless you in the best kind of ways both now and forever.

DEAR LORD, I DON'T WANT TO BE LIKE THOSE WHO LOVE TO SIN AND REJECT YOU AND YOUR GOOD WAYS. I WANT ALL MY HAPPINESS AND JOY TO COME FROM FOLLOWING YOU, RESTING IN YOU, AND WAITING ON YOU! AMEN.

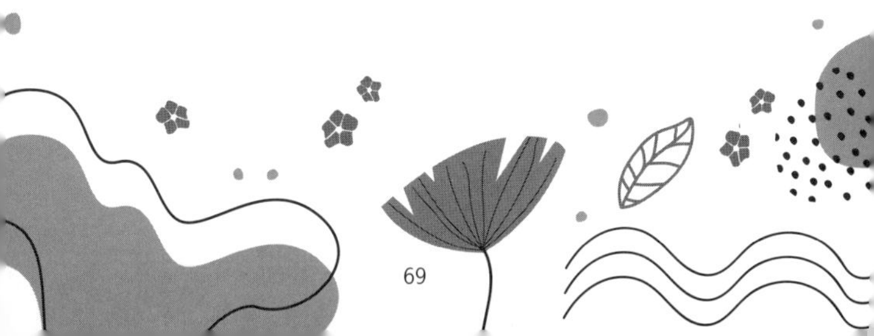

WONDERFUL CREATION

"But ask the animals, and they will teach you, or the birds in the sky, and they will tell you; or speak to the earth, and it will teach you, or let the fish in the sea inform you. Which of all these does not know that the hand of the Lord *has done this? In his hand is the life of every creature and the breath of all mankind."*

Job 12:7–10 NIV

Be intentional about spending quiet time with God outside, in His wonderful creation. In your backyard or at a park, in the mountains or at the beach, in the woods or near a river—God's creation and His creatures give us so many reasons to praise Him! He made every good thing, and His power and goodness are evident when we focus on all that He has designed and created.

I PRAISE YOU FOR HOW AWESOME YOU ARE, GOD! YOUR CREATION IS AMAZING, AND I'M GLAD YOU BLESS US WITH SO MANY BEAUTIFUL PLACES AND CREATURES IN THIS WORLD. AMEN.

WALK WITH WISE PEOPLE

Whoever walks with the wise becomes wise,
but the companion of fools will suffer harm.

PROVERBS 13:20 ESV

Think about the people you admire most. What is special about them? Is it their careers? Is it their talents? Is it how they treat you and other people? It's a great idea to get in the habit now of asking sincere questions to the adults you admire. Ask them how they got into the job or activities they are in. Ask what it was like to endure the hard things they've gone through in life. Be willing to have deep conversations so that you can learn important lessons from those who are older and wiser than you.

PLEASE SHOW ME THE WISE PEOPLE YOU WANT ME TO ADMIRE AND LEARN FROM, LORD. HELP ME TO DEVELOP MENTORING RELATIONSHIPS WITH THEM AND TO HAVE GOOD CONVERSATIONS. I AM SO THANKFUL THAT I CAN LOOK UP TO THEM. AMEN.

GOD TAKES AWAY TRANSGRESSIONS

The Lord is compassionate and gracious, slow to anger, abounding in love. . . . For as high as the heavens are above the earth, so great is his love for those who fear him; as far as the east is from the west, so far has he removed our transgressions from us. As a father has compassion on his children, so the Lord has compassion on those who fear him.

Psalm 103:8, 11–13 NIV

No one but the one true God can take away sins, and He does it in the best and biggest way. He takes your sins away from you as far as possible—as far as the east is from the west. That's incredible! In your quiet time today, focus on being thankful for God taking away your sins. Let relief and peace fill you to overflowing with praise to our heavenly Father.

DEAR FATHER, I CAN NEVER THANK YOU ENOUGH FOR TAKING AWAY MY SINS BECAUSE I TRUST IN JESUS AS MY SAVIOR. WITH GRATITUDE, I WANT TO LOVE AND RESPECT AND OBEY YOU ALL MY DAYS! AMEN.

EVERY SINGLE GOOD THING

Whatever is good and perfect is a gift coming down to us from God our Father, who created all the lights in the heavens. He never changes.

James 1:17 NLT

Do you ever stop and look around and tell God thanks for all the simple blessings you're experiencing right this very moment? Try it right now. Thank Him for the ability to read this sentence and even just to take another breath.

The Bible tells us that every good gift is from our Father God in heaven and that "He is the One who gives life and breath and everything to everyone" (Acts 17:25 NLV). We can choose to focus on even the smallest of blessings every day and be full of thanks and praise to God—and that should make us the happiest kind of people who love to share God's joy with others!

HEAVENLY FATHER, THANK YOU SO MUCH FOR EVEN THE BLESSINGS THAT SEEM THE SMALLEST IN MY LIFE. I CONSTANTLY WANT TO REMEMBER THAT EVERY GOOD THING COMES FROM YOU. HELP ME TO SHARE THIS TRUTH WITH OTHERS, PLUS ALL THE JOY THAT COMES FROM BEING YOUR CHILD.

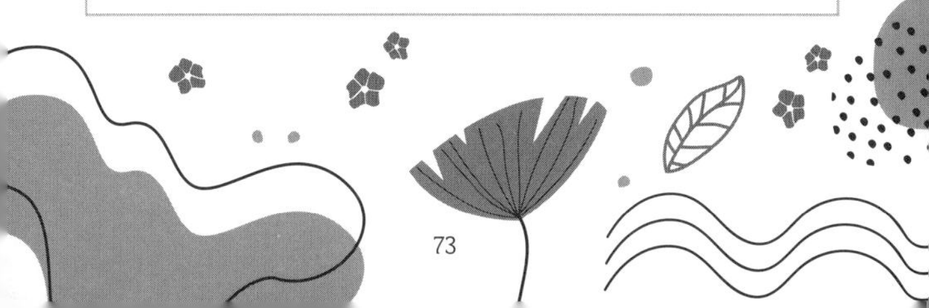

FIGHT WITH GOD'S ARMOR ON

For we are not fighting against flesh-and-blood enemies, but against evil rulers and authorities of the unseen world, against mighty powers in this dark world, and against evil spirits in the heavenly places. Therefore, put on every piece of God's armor so you will be able to resist the enemy in the time of evil. Then after the battle you will still be standing firm. Stand your ground, putting on the belt of truth and the body armor of God's righteousness. For shoes, put on the peace that comes from the Good News so that you will be fully prepared. In addition to all of these, hold up the shield of faith to stop the fiery arrows of the devil. Put on salvation as your helmet, and take the sword of the Spirit, which is the word of God.

Ephesians 6:12–17 NLT

We are in a spiritual battle in this world, but we don't need to fear anything when we have God's protection. In your quiet time today, focus on these verses from the book of Ephesians, and ask God to teach you more about what it means to wear His armor every day.

ALMIGHTY GOD, I WANT TO WEAR ALL THE ARMOR, ALL THE SPIRITUAL GEAR, THAT YOUR WORD DESCRIBES. HELP ME TO LEARN AND TRUST YOU MORE AND MORE FOR STRENGTH AND PROTECTION. AMEN.

WHAT'S YOUR NAME LIKE?

A good name is to be chosen instead of many riches.

PROVERBS 22:1 NLV

In your quiet time today, think about your reputation. When people hear your name, what first comes to their minds? Do you want them to think of you in good ways or bad ways? Do you want to be known for things like laziness or lying or rudeness or getting into trouble? Or do you want to be known for living for Jesus and things like doing your best and being loving, honest, fair, kind, and worthy of respect?

Choose now, while you are young, to always do your very best to have a good name your whole life. It doesn't mean you will be perfect, but it means you will obey God's ways of love and fairness and honesty—and you will quickly want to make things right when you make a mistake.

DEAR GOD, I WANT TO BE KNOWN FOR GOOD CHARACTER AND GOOD REPUTATION BECAUSE I LOVE AND FOLLOW YOU. I WANT A GOOD NAME, AND I WANT TO POINT PEOPLE TOWARD PRAISING YOUR NAME ABOVE ALL! AMEN.

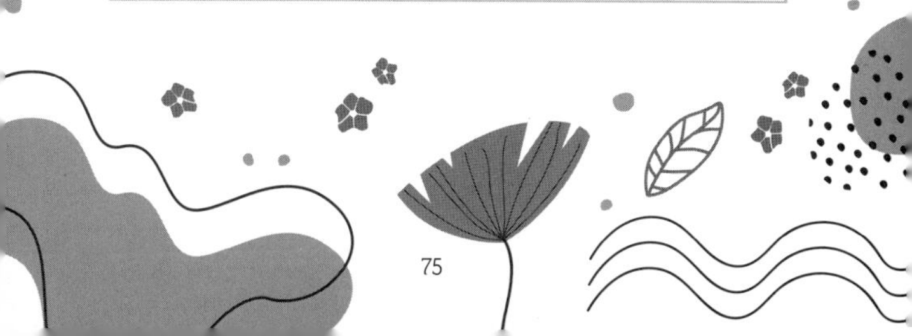

GOD WILL SUPPLY

God will supply every need of yours according to his riches in glory in Christ Jesus.

PHILIPPIANS 4:19 ESV

If you or your family are in the middle of a financial struggle, waiting and praying and wondering how God is going to provide, let this scripture calm your heart and comfort you in your quiet time today. God has promised to supply all your needs. Never forget that. And He knows exactly what you need before you even ask Him (Matthew 6:8). So don't fuss and fret. Keep being faithful and obedient to God and His Word, and seek His will, and then watch how He provides and blesses in amazing ways.

HEAVENLY FATHER, I WANT TO FULLY FOCUS ON HOW MUCH YOU LOVE ME AND HOW CAPABLE YOU ARE TO PROVIDE ABOVE AND BEYOND WHAT I CAN EVEN IMAGINE. THANK YOU FOR KNOWING MY NEEDS AND MY FAMILY'S NEEDS. THANK YOU FOR MEETING THOSE NEEDS—PLUS PROVIDING MANY EXTRA BLESSINGS ON TOP! AMEN.

GOD WILL GIVE YOU WISDOM

If you need wisdom, ask our generous God, and he will give it to you. He will not rebuke you for asking. But when you ask him, be sure that your faith is in God alone. Do not waver, for a person with divided loyalty is as unsettled as a wave of the sea that is blown and tossed by the wind. Such people should not expect to receive anything from the Lord. Their loyalty is divided between God and the world, and they are unstable in everything they do.

James 1:5–8 NLT

In everything you do and think and say throughout your day, God wants to help you. He wants you to ask for and use His wisdom as you make choices and learn and mature. And He never wants you to doubt His wisdom. He doesn't want you to be like a wave that's pushed around by the sea. He wants you to use His wisdom to be strong and stable, ready and able to do the good things He planned for you when He created you.

DEAR GOD, PLEASE GIVE ME YOUR WISDOM FOR EVERYTHING IN MY LIFE. HELP ME TO TRUST YOU AND TO USE THAT WISDOM EXACTLY THE WAY YOU WANT ME TO. AMEN.

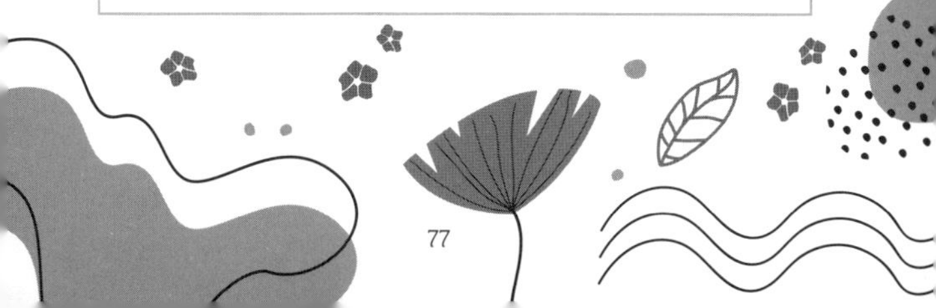

YOU BRING JOY TO GOD

"The Lord your God is with you, a Powerful One Who wins the battle. He will have much joy over you. With His love He will give you new life. He will have joy over you with loud singing."

ZEPHANIAH 3:17 NLV

Think of the last time you made someone smile. Doesn't it feel good to make someone happy? In your quiet time today, thank God for those opportunities to encourage and bring joy to people in your life. And then think about making God happy and seeing Him smile too. He does smile over you, you know. You bring Him joy simply by being you. He loves you so much that He sent His only Son to die and pay the price for your sin so that He could have a relationship with you.

DEAR GOD, IT'S AMAZING HOW MIGHTY YOU ARE OVER ALL OF CREATION, AND YOU ALSO SEE ME! AND YOU DON'T JUST SEE ME, BUT YOU LOVE ME AND YOU SMILE AND HAVE JOY BECAUSE OF ME. WOW! I WANT TO GROW CLOSER TO YOU EVERY DAY! AMEN.

THINK POSITIVELY, PART 1

Fix your thoughts on what is true, and honorable, and right, and pure, and lovely, and admirable. Think about things that are excellent and worthy of praise.

PHILIPPIANS 4:8 NLT

On days when everything seems to be going wrong, our first thoughts aren't usually happy, thankful ones. But God wants us to get rid of negative and evil thoughts and keep our minds thinking positively on good and pure things.

When we focus on praise and gratitude to God most of all (and on the many things that are right and true in our lives), we keep our thoughts in the best places. When negative and nasty thoughts try to take over our minds, we can ignore and reject them and then replace them with thoughts that are focused on God's goodness and love.

DEAR GOD, PLEASE HELP ME TO KEEP MY BRAIN THINKING ABOUT WHAT IS GOOD FOR ME—MOST OF ALL YOU, BECAUSE YOU ARE SO AWESOME! AMEN.

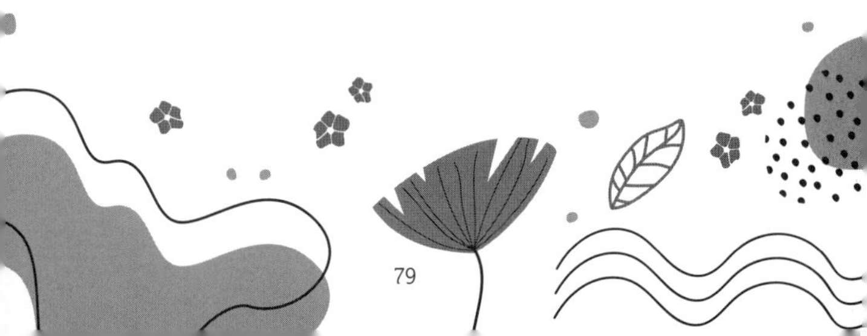

THINK POSITIVELY, PART 2

Do not conform to the pattern of this world, but be transformed by the renewing of your mind. Then you will be able to test and approve what God's will is—his good, pleasing and perfect will.

Romans 12:2 NIV

God wants to give you a new mind full of thoughts that are focused on Him and that are wise and right and true. Check out these verses:

- "If your sinful old self is the boss over your mind, it leads to death. But if the Holy Spirit is the boss over your mind, it leads to life and peace" (Romans 8:6 NLV).
- "You keep him in perfect peace whose mind is stayed on you, because he trusts in you" (Isaiah 26:3 ESV).
- "If then you have been raised with Christ, keep looking for the good things of heaven. This is where Christ is seated on the right side of God. Keep your minds thinking about things in heaven" (Colossians 3:1–2 NLV).

DEAR GOD, PLEASE GIVE ME A NEW MIND THROUGH YOUR HOLY SPIRIT. I WANT TO THINK ABOUT YOU AND FOLLOW YOU MORE THAN ANYTHING IN THIS WORLD! AMEN.

LET NOTHING MOVE YOU

Therefore, my dear brothers and sisters, stand firm. Let nothing move you. Always give yourselves fully to the work of the Lord.

1 Corinthians 15:58 NIV

God doesn't want us to be wobbly and weak in our faith. He wants us to stand firm. We aren't supposed to let anything move us.

We need to evaluate on a regular basis whether we have stuff going on in our lives that weakens our faith and tempts us to move away from God. Do we need to ditch any bad habits or activities that aren't honoring to God? Are we holding on to any sin? Are we giving ourselves fully to God and the good works He has planned for us? That's how we keep ourselves standing firm and immovable in our faith.

HEAVENLY FATHER, I WANT TO STAND STRONG AND IMMOVABLE IN MY FAITH IN YOU AND IN MY WILLINGNESS TO DO WHATEVER WORK YOU ASK OF ME. PLEASE HELP ME TO RID MY LIFE OF ANYTHING THAT WEAKENS MY FAITH AND THREATENS MY RELATIONSHIP WITH YOU. AMEN.

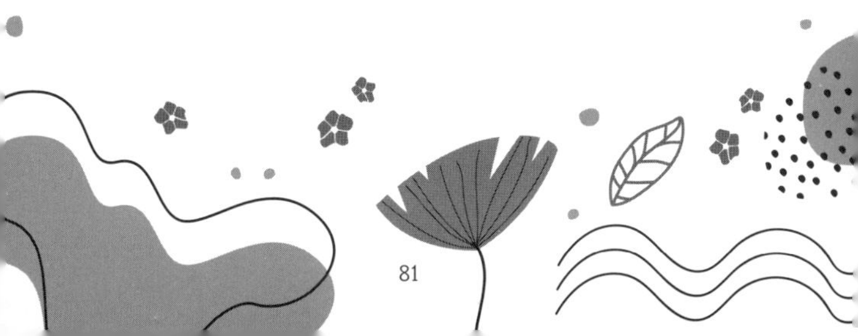

WHEN BAD THINGS HAPPEN

We know that we are children of God and that the world around us is under the control of the evil one. And we know that the Son of God has come, and he has given us understanding so that we can know the true God. And now we live in fellowship with the true God because we live in fellowship with his Son, Jesus Christ. He is the only true God, and he is eternal life. Dear children, keep away from anything that might take God's place in your hearts.

1 JOHN 5:19–21 NLT

Why do bad things happen? We all wonder about this sometimes—especially when we're in the middle of something horrible ourselves. Unfortunately, the bad things shouldn't surprise us, because the Bible is clear that the whole world is under the power of the evil one, Satan—a.k.a. the devil. But for all of us who believe in Jesus as our one true Savior, we belong to God—so the devil can never, ever defeat us. The devil can attack us and hurt us in this world, but ultimately we have victory because God gives us life that lasts forever no matter what.

DEAR GOD, PLEASE GIVE ME EXTRA LOVE AND WISDOM WHEN BAD THINGS HAPPEN AND I'M HURTING AND CONFUSED. IN EVERY CIRCUMSTANCE, I CHOOSE TO TRUST THAT WITH JESUS AS MY SAVIOR, NO MATTER WHAT HAPPENS TO ME, YOU GIVE ME LIFE THAT LASTS FOREVER! AMEN.

LET YOUR ROOTS GROW DEEP

And now, just as you accepted Christ Jesus as your Lord, you must continue to follow him. Let your roots grow down into him, and let your lives be built on him. Then your faith will grow strong in the truth you were taught, and you will overflow with thankfulness. Don't let anyone capture you with empty philosophies and high-sounding nonsense that come from human thinking and from the spiritual powers of this world, rather than from Christ.

COLOSSIANS 2:6–8 NLT

Focus on this passage from Colossians in your quiet time today. Let it motivate you in your relationship with Jesus every day. The deeper your roots grow into Him, the sturdier your life is built on Him and the stronger your faith is in Him. And with deep roots, a sturdy life, and strong faith, the better you can live a truly joyful life, accomplishing all the good plans God has for you. You will still have hard times, of course, but they won't ever be able to completely overwhelm you. When you're strong in relationship with Jesus, you're ready to stand against any spiritual attack.

DEAR GOD, HELP ME TO BE LIKE THE STURDIEST, TALLEST TREE WITH MY ROOTS GROWING STRONG AND DEEP INTO YOU. AMEN.

DEALING WITH TOUGH PEOPLE

Open your heart to teaching,
and your ears to words of much learning.
PROVERBS 23:12 NLV

You're going to have some teachers and leaders and coaches in your life who are wonderful to learn from—and some who definitely aren't. Maybe right now you can think of a particular someone who is just *so hard* to learn from. Maybe his or her rules and assignments and expectations all seem too much. Maybe his or her attitude is constantly discouraging.

God cares about your situation. Ask Him to help things get better—whether it's that a teacher or coach needs to change his or her ways, or perhaps it's you who needs to adapt. Let God show you how to communicate effectively with the teacher or coach as you do your best to manage a tough situation.

DEAR GOD, PLEASE HELP ME TO MAKE IT THROUGH THIS TOUGH TIME WITH A DIFFICULT LEADER. HELP ME TO DO MY BEST AND SHOW RESPECT, EVEN WHEN I DON'T FEEL LIKE IT. PLEASE HELP THINGS TO GET BETTER AND MAKE ME STRONGER AND WISER BECAUSE OF THIS SITUATION. AMEN.

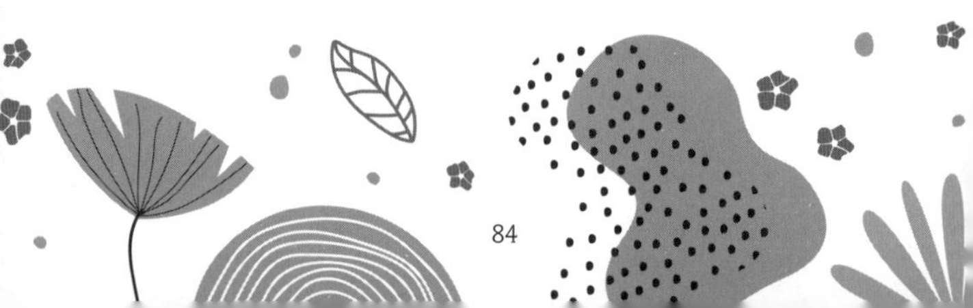

THE WAY YOU GIVE

If you give to others, you will be given a full amount in return. It will be packed down, shaken together, and spilling over into your lap. The way you treat others is the way you will be treated.

Luke 6:38 CEV

Think about all the ways you give in your quiet time today. Jesus clearly taught that we are supposed to be generous and willing to share what we've been blessed with. If we're selfish and keep all our blessings for ourselves, we won't see how God loves to give more and more to those who love to share what they have.

Aren't you grateful for the givers in your life? Who are the most generous people you can think of? Who are the most selfish? Who do you want to be like? Most of all, do you want to obey what Jesus taught about giving? These are good questions for all of us to ask ourselves regularly.

DEAR JESUS, THANK YOU FOR MY MANY BLESSINGS. I DON'T WANT TO BE SELFISH AND GREEDY. HELP ME TO LOVE GIVING AND SHARING WITH OTHERS AS YOU TAUGHT. AMEN.

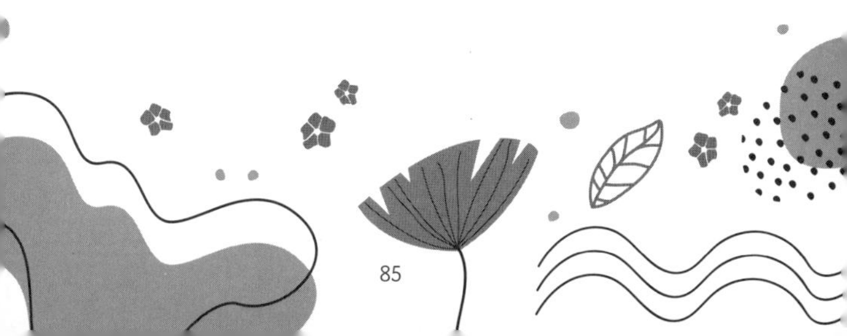

DON'T ENVY THOSE WHO DO WRONG

Don't worry about the wicked or envy those who do wrong. For like grass, they soon fade away. Like spring flowers, they soon wither. Trust in the LORD and do good. Then you will live safely in the land and prosper. Take delight in the LORD, and he will give you your heart's desires.

PSALM 37:1–4 NLT

It seems like people who choose to do wrong things are everywhere. And honestly, sometimes it even looks fun and harmless to go along with whatever seems popular—even if you know deep down that a lot of what is popular is wrong. It takes a lot of strength and courage not to join in with those who do wrong, especially if you're feeling pressure from those you thought were your close friends. But God promises that if you trust Him and do good, you will have everything you need—and He will give you the things that make you happy because you are happy in Him first!

DEAR GOD, PLEASE HELP ME TO STAND STRONG UNDER PEER PRESSURE. I DON'T WANT TO ENVY OR TRY TO BE LIKE THOSE WHO DO WRONG. I WANT TO DO WHAT MAKES YOU HAPPY—AND I TRUST THAT'S THE BEST WAY FOR ME TO LIVE AND HAVE REAL JOY. AMEN.

WORSHIP ALL THE TIME

Shout for joy to the LORD, all the earth. Worship the LORD with gladness; come before him with joyful songs. Know that the LORD is God. It is he who made us, and we are his; we are his people, the sheep of his pasture. Enter his gates with thanksgiving and his courts with praise; give thanks to him and praise his name. For the LORD is good and his love endures forever; his faithfulness continues through all generations.

PSALM 100 NIV

With psalms like this and with your favorite songs you've learned about God, worship Him! Anytime, anywhere—even when you need to be quiet—you can focus on praising God in your mind and immediately be filled with goodness and joy.

ALMIGHTY GOD, YOU ALONE ARE WORTHY OF WORSHIP! I WANT TO PRAISE YOU AT ALL TIMES EVERYWHERE I GO, IN EVERYTHING I DO! YOU ARE SO GOOD AND SO AMAZING! AMEN.

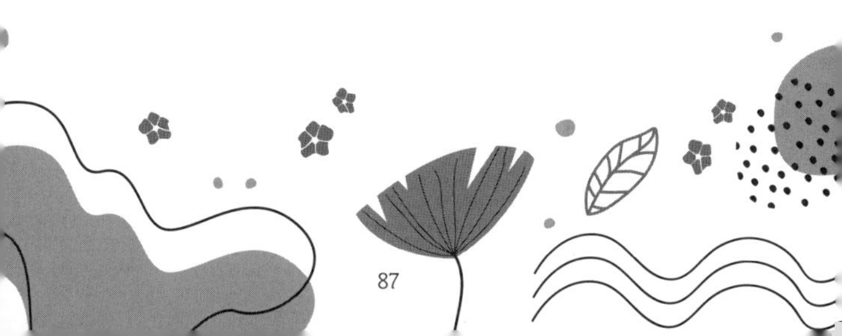

LIFE WILL CHANGE, BUT GOD WON'T

"For I the Lord do not change."

Malachi 3:6 ESV

In your quiet time today, think about change. How much change have you experienced lately? Life has so many changes year to year, sometimes even day to day. There are major changes and minor ones—changes with friends and in your family, changes at home and at school.

Change can be exciting if you love new things and new adventures, but change can feel strange or sad or overwhelming at times too. So it's wonderful to remember that God promises that He never changes. He is our one constant no matter what new things are going on in our lives. Hebrews 13:8 (ESV) says, "Jesus is the same yesterday and today and forever." That's amazing!

DEAR GOD, THANK YOU FOR BEING A CONSTANT COMFORT AND HELP TO ME! YOU ARE MY STEADY, UNCHANGING STRENGTH, AND I LOVE YOU! AMEN.

DO YOU FEEL ALL ALONE?

Everyone abandoned me. May it not be counted against them. But the Lord stood with me and gave me strength so that I might preach the Good News in its entirety for all the Gentiles to hear. And he rescued me from certain death. Yes, and the Lord will deliver me from every evil attack and will bring me safely into his heavenly Kingdom. All glory to God forever and ever!

2 TIMOTHY 4:16–18 NLT

When you feel all alone, with no one to help you, you can read and remember these words that Paul wrote in the Bible. Even though no other person was there to help, God Himself was with Paul. God protected him and gave him power. Paul realized that no matter what happened on earth, God would someday welcome him into heaven forever. Paul wrote these words in his letter to Timothy to teach him about God's protection, but it's also for us to trust today too.

I TRUST THAT NO MATTER WHAT HAPPENS HERE IN THIS WORLD, LORD, YOU WILL ALWAYS BE WITH ME AND KEEP ME SAFE. SOMEDAY YOU ARE GOING TO BRING ME INTO YOUR PERFECT PARADISE IN HEAVEN TO BE WITH YOU! IN THE MEANTIME, HELP ME TO LIVE OUT YOUR AWESOME PLANS FOR ME HERE ON EARTH. AMEN.

IF SAUL COULD CHANGE, ANYONE CAN

Now as he went on his way, he approached Damascus, and suddenly a light from heaven shone around him. And falling to the ground, he heard a voice saying to him, "Saul, Saul, why are you persecuting me?" And he said, "Who are you, Lord?" And he said, "I am Jesus, whom you are persecuting. But rise and enter the city, and you will be told what you are to do."

ACTS 9:3–6 ESV

If you read the story of Saul (later Paul) in the New Testament, you'll be amazed at how Jesus totally turned his life around. Saul had hated Christians to the point of killing them, and then God confronted him and worked a miracle in Saul's life. Saul then became one of the greatest followers of Jesus. If God can do this for someone like Saul, he can do it for anyone, so keep on praying for those who need a miracle too.

DEAR GOD, I PRAY FOR THESE PEOPLE RIGHT NOW ____________, WHO NEED AN INCREDIBLE MIRACLE TO LEARN TO LOVE AND FOLLOW YOU. I BELIEVE YOU CAN MAKE IT HAPPEN! AMEN.

GOD CAN MAKE IT GOOD

Joseph replied, "Don't be afraid of me. Am I God, that I can punish you? You intended to harm me, but God intended it all for good. He brought me to this position so I could save the lives of many people. No, don't be afraid. I will continue to take care of you and your children." So he reassured them by speaking kindly to them.

GENESIS 50:19–21 NLT

Don't ever forget that God can take the very worst of situations and turn them upside down. He can take anyone's evil plans toward you and work them out for your good. Think about Joseph in the Bible. It doesn't get much worse than being sold by your siblings into slavery in another country. But read the whole story of Joseph's life and see how God blessed Joseph and brought good out of that awful experience.

Whatever you are going through today, no matter how hard it is, choose to be loyal and obedient to God like Joseph was, and in His perfect timing God will surely bless you for your faithfulness.

HEAVENLY FATHER, THANK YOU FOR JOSEPH'S STORY TO INSPIRE AND ENCOURAGE ME TO KEEP BEING FAITHFUL TO YOU EVEN IN THE VERY WORST KINDS OF SITUATIONS AND INJUSTICE. YOU CAN TAKE ANYTHING THAT'S MEANT TO HARM ME AND TURN IT INTO SOMETHING GOOD. I BELIEVE THAT, AND I TRUST YOU! AMEN.

HOW LONG?

I wait for the Lord, my soul waits, and in his word I hope.

Psalm 130:5 ESV

Sometimes it's *so hard* to wait on God's answers to prayer. The prophet Habakkuk in the Bible was impatient too. He prayed, "How long, O Lord, must I call for help? But you do not listen! . . . Must I forever see these evil deeds? Why must I watch all this misery? Wherever I look, I see destruction and violence. I am surrounded by people who love to argue and fight. The law has become paralyzed, and there is no justice in the courts. The wicked far outnumber the righteous, so that justice has become perverted" (Habakkuk 1:2–4 NLT).

We can learn from God's response that our human minds can't fully comprehend what God is doing while we wait for Him to answer prayer. He said to Habakkuk, "Look around at the nations; look and be amazed! For I am doing something in your own day, something you wouldn't believe even if someone told you about it" (Habakkuk 1:5 NLT).

DEAR GOD, HELP ME TO REMEMBER THAT YOU DO THINGS MY MIND CAN NEVER FULLY UNDERSTAND. YOU ARE WORKING OUT YOUR PLANS IN EXACTLY THE RIGHT WAYS. I CHOOSE TO TRUST YOU NO MATTER WHAT. AMEN.

CHILL

Since God chose you to be the holy people he loves, you must clothe yourselves with tenderhearted mercy, kindness, humility, gentleness, and patience. Make allowance for each other's faults, and forgive anyone who offends you. Remember, the Lord forgave you, so you must forgive others. Above all, clothe yourselves with love, which binds us all together in perfect harmony. And let the peace that comes from Christ rule in your hearts. For as members of one body you are called to live in peace.

COLOSSIANS 3:12–15 NLT

The last time you were mad at someone, did it help to explode in anger at the person? Or did it make things worse? When people are driving you crazy, you definitely need quiet time with God. Let Him chill out your anger and calm your soul. Let Him show You through His Word how He wants you to act toward others—with an abundance of patience, grace, forgiveness, and love, just like He's always giving you.

DEAR GOD, PLEASE HELP ME TO CHILL OUT WHEN I'M MAD. KEEP ME CALM WITH YOUR PEACE. HELP ME TO TREAT OTHERS WITH LOVE LIKE YOU DO. AMEN.

GOD CAN HANDLE HARD QUESTIONS

"Will the Lord reject forever? Will he never show his favor again? Has his unfailing love vanished forever? Has his promise failed for all time? Has God forgotten to be merciful? Has he in anger withheld his compassion?" Then I thought, "To this I will appeal: the years when the Most High stretched out his right hand. I will remember the deeds of the Lord*; yes, I will remember your miracles of long ago. I will consider all your works and meditate on all your mighty deeds."*

Psalm 77:7–12 niv

If you're hurting and feel hopeless today, it's okay to use your quiet time to ask God hard questions and tell Him all about your sadness and pain—just like the writer of this psalm did. Often, in difficult times, we wonder where God is and if He has forgotten to take care of us. So we need to focus on remembering all the good things our loving heavenly Father has done for us in the past and in His perfect timing, and then trust that He will continue to bring goodness to our lives.

DEAR GOD, I'M SAD AND HURTING RIGHT NOW. I ADMIT I HAVE LOTS OF QUESTIONS BECAUSE I DON'T FULLY UNDERSTAND YOU. BUT I CHOOSE TO TRUST YOU ANYWAY. I WANT TO FOCUS ON YOUR GOODNESS IN MY LIFE IN THE PAST—AND THEN TRUST THAT YOU WILL HELP ME AND BLESS ME TODAY AND IN THE FUTURE, JUST LIKE YOU ALWAYS HAVE. AMEN.

NEVER CRUSHED OR DESTROYED

We are afflicted in every way, but not crushed; perplexed, but not driven to despair; persecuted, but not forsaken; struck down, but not destroyed.

2 Corinthians 4:8–9 ESV

Maybe you're in the middle of weeks or perhaps even months when everything seems to be going wrong. You might be feeling so discouraged that you begin to wonder if God is ever going to step in to rescue you, or at the very least protect you from any more trouble.

This scripture in 2 Corinthians promises that no matter how discouraged you feel, no matter how long you've been waiting for rescue, God will never let you get to a point where you cannot handle your discouragement. Sometimes He will wait till the very last moment, but He will always provide a way out. He lets us experience hard things at times to teach us lessons and show us how strong we can be when we depend on Him.

HEAVENLY FATHER, PLEASE HELP ME TO KEEP HANGING IN THERE WHEN I FEEL DISCOURAGED AND CONFUSED AND IN PAIN FOR SUCH A LONG TIME. I KNOW YOU NEVER ABANDON ME, AND YOU HAVE GOOD PLANS AND BLESSINGS IN STORE FOR ME. AMEN.

WHEN GOD IS ASKING YOU TO WAIT

When God made a promise to Abraham,
He made that promise in His own name because
no one was greater. He said, "I will make you
happy in so many ways. For sure, I will give you
many children." Abraham was willing to wait
and God gave to him what He had promised.

Hebrews 6:13–15 NLV

Have you been praying for something but nothing seems to be happening? When God asks us to wait, it's sometimes hard to stay patient. So we need to look to the examples of others who have waited on God and then seen His promises come true. Like Abraham, we need to be willing to wait and let God work in His perfect timing.

DEAR GOD, I STRUGGLE WITH BEING PATIENT SOMETIMES. I WANT WHAT I WANT RIGHT NOW, AND I DON'T LIKE TO WAIT. PLEASE HELP ME WITH THIS. I NEED TO DO BETTER AT TRUSTING IN YOUR TIMING INSTEAD OF WANTING THINGS TO WORK OUT ON MY OWN TIMELINE. AMEN.

LET GOD HANDLE JUSTICE

Do not repay anyone evil for evil. Be careful to do what is right in the eyes of everyone. If it is possible, as far as it depends on you, live at peace with everyone. Do not take revenge, my dear friends, but leave room for God's wrath.

ROMANS 12:17–19 NIV

When we're mistreated, we're far better off to let God handle the situation than to try to handle it ourselves. God loves us so much more than even our very best family and friends. We can trust Him to take care of our needs and bring justice when we've been wronged. That doesn't mean we have to be doormats who get walked on. That doesn't mean God never asks us to do something to stand up for ourselves. It means we humbly ask for God's help and His plans for true justice more than we want our own way and our own ideas of justice.

We ask God to guide us and tell us when to speak up and when to be quiet, when to act and when to be still. God knows and sees everything, and He gets angry at injustice too! His justice and goodness will always prevail, not always in the timing we'd like, but always according to His perfect schedule.

DEAR GOD, PLEASE CALM MY SOUL AND GIVE ME YOUR WISDOM. HELP ME TO LET YOU HANDLE UNJUST SITUATIONS. YOU WILL DELIVER PERFECT JUSTICE EVERY TIME. AMEN.

LOVING ENEMIES?

"You have heard that it was said, 'You shall love your neighbor and hate your enemy.' But I say to you, Love your enemies and pray for those who persecute you, so that you may be sons of your Father who is in heaven."

MATTHEW 5:43–45 ESV

Use your quiet time today to do one of the hardest things Jesus will ever ask us to do: love our enemies and pray for those who try to hurt us. Even though it's so very hard to do, Jesus will help us. And when we do love and pray for our enemies, we are acting like true children of God.

> JESUS, I ADMIT THAT I DON'T LIKE THIS COMMAND VERY MUCH. IT'S SO HARD TO LISTEN TO YOUR INSTRUCTION ABOUT LOVING AND PRAYING FOR THE PEOPLE WHO MISTREAT ME! BUT I WANT TO DO MY BEST AT THIS WITH YOUR HELP BECAUSE I LOVE YOU AND WANT TO OBEY YOU. IT'S ONLY BY YOUR GRACE AND POWER THAT I CAN PRAY FOR AND LOVE AND BLESS MY ENEMIES. I'M TRUSTING YOU TO HELP ME. I PRAY FOR THESE SPECIFIC PEOPLE RIGHT NOW:______________.

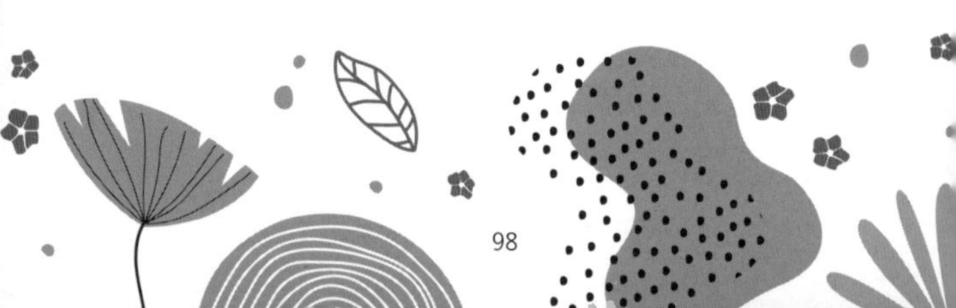

HIGH LOW

Is anyone among you suffering? Let him pray.
Is anyone cheerful? Let him sing praise.

James 5:13 ESV

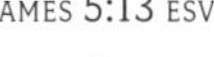

If you're ever stuck and not sure what to say to God in your quiet time with Him, try playing a game of "High Low." Tell Him the high or best part of your day. And then tell Him the low or worst part. Even though He was with you through it all, He loves for you to talk to Him about anything and everything. Invite God into your thoughts and feelings, knowing that He is already constantly present with you anyway and loves to be welcomed by you. When you're sharing about the different events of the day and how they made you feel, give any worries and fears and needs to God and praise Him for all the good things. He cares about every high and every low plus everything in between.

DEAR GOD, PLEASE HELP ME TO REMEMBER YOUR CONSTANT PRESENCE WITH ME. I WELCOME YOU INTO EVERY PART OF MY LIFE. I LOVE YOU AND NEED YOU SO MUCH! AMEN.

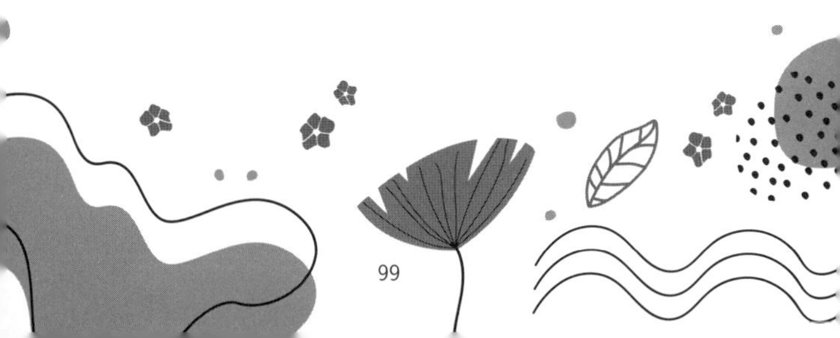

GOD'S PERFECT COMFORT

[God] comforts us in all our troubles, so that we can comfort those in any trouble with the comfort we ourselves receive from God. For just as we share abundantly in the sufferings of Christ, so also our comfort abounds through Christ. If we are distressed, it is for your comfort and salvation; if we are comforted, it is for your comfort, which produces in you patient endurance of the same sufferings we suffer.

2 Corinthians 1:4–6 niv

When you feel confused about hard or sad things in your life and in the world, spend time learning and soaking up the truth of this scripture. God will comfort you in the middle of painful times, and then you can comfort others with His love and care too. And one day, when Jesus returns to make all things new, you'll never have sadness or pain ever again.

DEAR GOD, HELP ME TO FEEL YOUR PERFECT COMFORT IN THE HARD TIMES, AND THEN HELP ME TO COMFORT AND ENCOURAGE OTHERS WHO ARE GOING THROUGH THE SAME KIND OF HARD THINGS. HELP ME TO POINT EVERYONE I CAN TO BE SAVED FROM THEIR SINS THROUGH FAITH IN JESUS CHRIST. AMEN.

WHEN YOU'RE MISTREATED

Ask God to bless everyone who mistreats you. Ask him to bless them and not to curse them. When others are happy, be happy with them, and when they are sad, be sad. Be friendly with everyone. Don't be proud and feel that you know more than others. Make friends with ordinary people. Don't mistreat someone who has mistreated you. But try to earn the respect of others, and do your best to live at peace with everyone.

ROMANS 12:14–18 CEV

If someone is mistreating you, make sure you spend extra quiet time with God. He will help you handle a hard situation in the right way. Ask for His wisdom and strength, and let His Word guide you.

DEAR GOD, YOU KNOW WHAT I'M GOING THROUGH. I SURE NEED YOUR HELP DEALING WITH THIS MISTREATMENT AND THE PERSON WHO IS RESPONSIBLE FOR IT. I DON'T KNOW EXACTLY WHAT TO DO, BUT I TRUST YOU TO SHOW ME. PLEASE GIVE ME WISDOM AND STRENGTH, AND HELP ME TO WORK THINGS OUT WITH LOVE AND PEACE. AMEN.

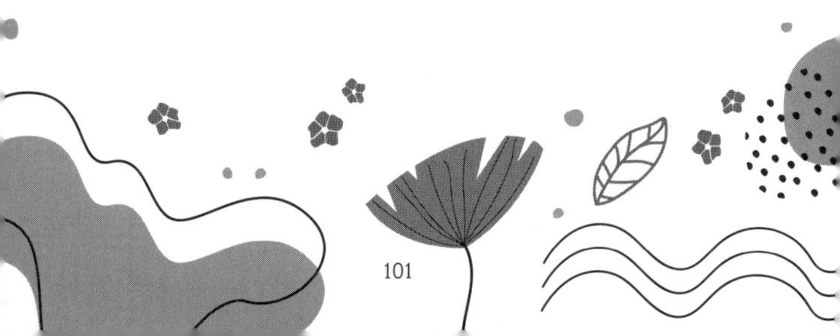

GOD'S GOT YOU

Let all who take refuge in you rejoice; let them sing joyful praises forever. Spread your protection over them, that all who love your name may be filled with joy. For you bless the godly, O LORD; you surround them with your shield of love.

PSALM 5:11–12 NLT

When you're worried and scared about troubles and problems and enemies in your life, remember that God protects you and provides for you. His Word promises that He shields you with His love.

You probably know what it's like to be out in the middle of a thunderstorm. Once you get to a safe place, you are so relieved! God is your refuge in every kind of storm life brings. Never forget that. Run to Him and receive protection and peace.

HEAVENLY FATHER, THANK YOU FOR COVERING ME WITH YOUR LOVE, BLESSING, PROTECTION, AND CARE. I DON'T KNOW WHAT I'D DO WITHOUT YOU! AMEN.

WALK LIKE YOU TALK

Let us not love with words or in talk only.
Let us love by what we do and in truth.

1 John 3:18 NLV

Do you hear people saying nice things in certain situations, but then their actions don't match—and are often pretty awful? We all can be guilty of that sometimes, and we need to be careful that we live honest lives—that we walk like we talk.

When you spend quiet time with God, learning about Him through prayer, reading the Bible, and listening for His voice, remember that what God says *always* matches what He does. His words are *always* true, and He proved His great love for all people by sending Jesus to pay for sin. Romans 5:8 (NLV) says, "God showed His love to us. While we were still sinners, Christ died for us."

DEAR JESUS, I WANT TO LOVE NOT JUST IN WORDS BUT IN EVERYTHING I DO. I WANT TO BE LIKE YOU! AMEN.

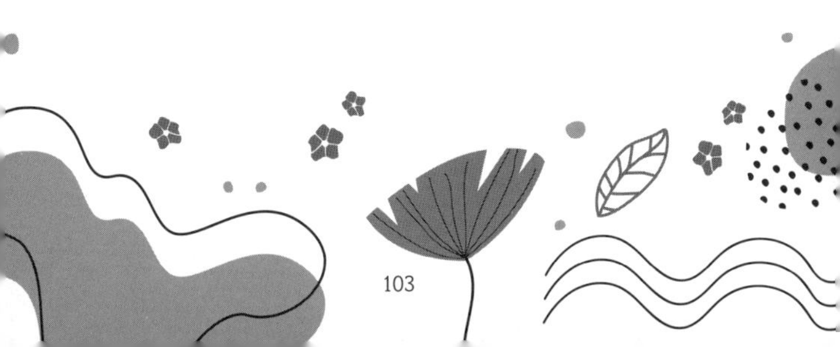

GOD REALLY IS ALWAYS THERE FOR YOU

God has said, "I will never fail you. I will never abandon you." So we can say with confidence, "The Lord is my helper, so I will have no fear. What can mere people do to me?"

Hebrews 13:5–6 NLT

People we love often say to us (and we say this to those we love too), "I'm always here for you." It's a great way to show love and loyalty and support. But sometimes, even though we try our hardest, it's just not possible to *always* be there for others, because we are human and not capable of being perfect. Only God can make that promise to absolutely, 100 percent, never, ever leave us. And He will never fail, not even accidentally, on that promise. Even if you don't feel Him with you at times, He is. Just keep calling out to Him in prayer and listening for Him, especially through His Word.

WHERE WOULD I BE WITHOUT YOU AS MY HELPER, LORD? I CAN'T THANK YOU ENOUGH FOR NEVER LEAVING ME ALONE. REMIND ME THAT I NEVER NEED TO BE AFRAID OF ANYTHING FOR YOU ARE ALWAYS WITH ME, ALWAYS HELPING ME, ALWAYS PROTECTING ME. AMEN.

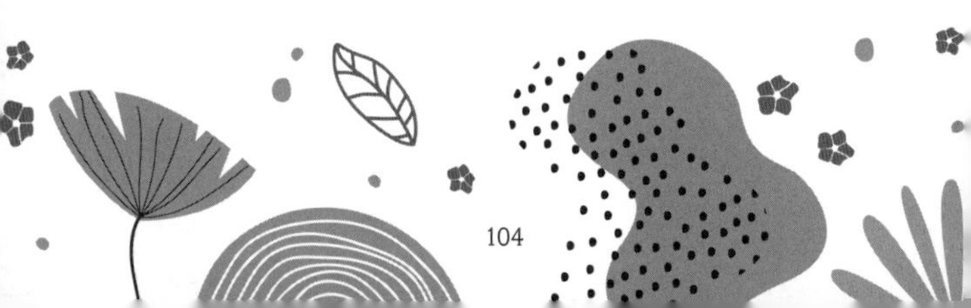

WHO ARE YOU TRYING TO PLEASE?

I'm not trying to win the approval of people, but of God. If pleasing people were my goal, I would not be Christ's servant.

Galatians 1:10 NLT

In your quiet time today, think about who you're trying to please and gain approval from. It's hard not to be a people pleaser when you desire to have friends and get along well with others. But God's Word tells us we shouldn't be looking for approval from people. We should instead look for God's approval above all.

If you start praying now to be a God pleaser and a servant of Jesus, you'll help yourself out for life: you won't be so worried about what other people think of you. You won't be inclined to give in to peer pressure. You'll be true to the unique, amazing person God designed you to be, and you'll follow the good plans He has for you. Yes, living for God's approval instead of people's approval isn't easy! But as you spend time with God and in His Word, He will help you keep your focus on Him. And at the same time, He'll be filling your life with the good-for-you relationships that you truly need.

DEAR GOD, I LOVE YOU MOST AND WANT TO PLEASE YOU, NOT OTHER PEOPLE. IT'S A STRUGGLE, THOUGH. I'M TRUSTING YOU WILL HELP ME. AMEN.

PRAY FOR ALL PEOPLE

Pray for all people. Ask God to help them; intercede on their behalf, and give thanks for them. Pray this way for kings and all who are in authority so that we can live peaceful and quiet lives marked by godliness and dignity. This is good and pleases God our Savior, who wants everyone to be saved and to understand the truth. For, there is one God and one Mediator who can reconcile God and humanity—the man Christ Jesus. He gave his life to purchase freedom for everyone.

1 TIMOTHY 2:1–6 NLT

It's impossible to run out of topics to pray about in your quiet time. Literally, everyone you know needs prayer. You don't have to know all their specific needs because God is so awesome He already knows them. But He wants you to talk to Him about those things in prayer because it shows you care about people and want others to depend on God for everything.

DEAR GOD, I'M GRATEFUL THAT YOU CARE ABOUT EVERY SINGLE PERSON, AND YOU KNOW EVERY SPECIFIC NEED. MOST OF ALL, I PRAY FOR MORE AND MORE PEOPLE TO BE SAVED FROM SIN BY CHOOSING TO BELIEVE IN JESUS CHRIST AS THEIR ONE AND ONLY SAVIOR FROM SIN. AMEN.

REAL, ETERNAL JOY

The hope of those who are right with God is joy, but the hope of the sinful comes to nothing. The way of the Lord is a strong-place to those who are faithful, but it destroys those who do wrong. Those who are right with God will never be shaken, but the sinful will not live in the land.

PROVERBS 10:28–30 NLV

Some people constantly turn away from Jesus and reject Him, yet they seem to have lives full of fun and happiness. That can be hard to watch, especially when we go through hard times that make us wonder if we should turn away from Jesus too. So we have to remember that real, eternal joy comes only from Jesus, and people who reject Him have hopeless futures. That's really sad. We should keep trying to point people to Jesus anyway, while keeping strong faith in Him no matter what to protect and bless us in the best ways both now and forever.

DEAR LORD, HELP ME TO KEEP LOOKING TO YOU, AND NOT AT THOSE WHO TURN AWAY FROM YOU AND REJECT YOU. I TRUST YOU. I KNOW THAT YOU LOVE ME AND WILL BLESS ME BOTH NOW AND FOREVER. AMEN.

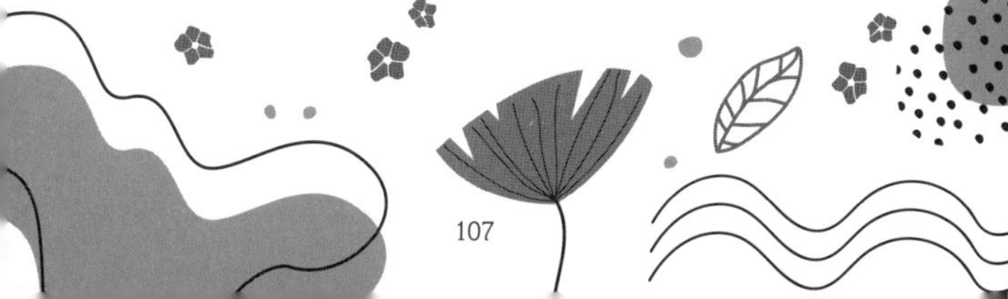

HE WON'T LET YOU DOWN

"God is not man, that he should lie, or a son of man, that he should change his mind. Has he said, and will he not do it? Or has he spoken, and will he not fulfill it?"

NUMBERS 23:19 ESV

People are going to let you down. It stinks, but it's true. No person can perfectly keep their promises because we are all human, we make mistakes, and things happen in life that we can't control. We should try our best to keep promises, of course—but only God can keep promises perfectly. Sometimes people even shamelessly lie to us, and that's awful, but God never will. He keeps His word, and we can trust Him.

DEAR GOD, SINCE PEOPLE HAVE LET ME DOWN, I SOMETIMES WONDER IF YOU WILL LET ME DOWN. PLEASE REMIND ME THAT YOU ARE THE PERFECT PROMISE KEEPER. YOU DON'T EVER LIE OR BREAK YOUR PROMISES. I CAN ALWAYS HOPE AND TRUST IN YOU. AMEN.

INSULTED BUT BLESSED

Trials make you partners with Christ in his suffering, so that you will have the wonderful joy of seeing his glory when it is revealed to all the world. If you are insulted because you bear the name of Christ, you will be blessed, for the glorious Spirit of God rests upon you.

1 Peter 4:13–14 NLT

You're going to get insulted for being a Christian and doing your best to obey God's Word and His ways. Maybe you already have. What's popular in the world is often opposite of what God's Word says is good and right. And when you don't go along with what's popular, there's a good chance you're going to get made fun of. It's not easy, but you can handle it and rise above it.

You are strong and brave because the Holy Spirit is in you! Keep on doing your best to obey Jesus and follow Him. He promises to bless you, and His Holy Spirit will never, ever leave you.

DEAR JESUS, I'LL FOLLOW YOU AND BE HAPPY TO BE CALLED A CHRISTIAN NO MATTER WHAT ANYONE ELSE SAYS ABOUT ME. YOU MAKE ME STRONG AND COURAGEOUS, AND YOU FILL MY LIFE WITH BLESSINGS. THANK YOU! AMEN.

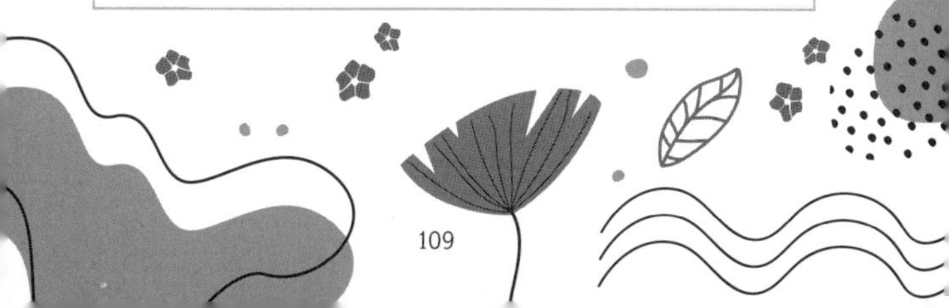

BE PROUD OF WHAT GOD DOES

If anyone wants to be proud, he should be proud of what the Lord has done. It is not what a man thinks and says of himself that is important. It is what God thinks of him.

2 Corinthians 10:17–18 NLV

When we reach a goal or accomplish something we've been working hard at, of course we feel happy and excited. We want to celebrate, and that's wonderful! However, we also need to remember to give God credit for every cool thing we do. That's a great way to stay humble and never become full of pride in ourselves. God is the one who deserves all the praise and worship because He is the one who created us and gives us our gifts and abilities in the first place.

DEAR GOD, I WANT TO BE PROUDER OF YOU THAN OF ANYTHING COOL I DO. YOU ARE THE ONE WHO GIVES ME EVERYTHING AND EVERY ABILITY TO ACCOMPLISH AMAZING THINGS. AND YOUR OPINION MATTERS MOST OF ALL. PLEASE HELP ME TO USE MY GIFTS WELL AND IN THE WAYS YOU WANT ME TO, ESPECIALLY TO SHARE YOUR LOVE AND TRUTH WITH OTHERS. AMEN.

LIFE AGAIN

We want you to know what will happen to the believers who have died so you will not grieve like people who have no hope. For since we believe that Jesus died and was raised to life again, we also believe that when Jesus returns, God will bring back with him the believers who have died.

1 Thessalonians 4:13–14 NLT

Maybe your quiet time is often full of missing someone and crying out to God in pain and confusion. When someone we love dies, it brings sadness and brokenness that can't ever be fully fixed here on earth. We ache because we miss our person beyond words, and it's hard not to be able to share our lives with them or hug them or even keep in touch by texting.

But for all who believe in Jesus as Savior, this life on earth is not all there is. We have new life and perfect heaven to look forward to, where we will spend forever with Jesus and all our loved ones who believe in Him too. If you have loved ones who don't yet believe in Jesus, keep praying for them and asking God how to show them His love and truth.

THANK YOU SO MUCH, JESUS, FOR THE PEACE AND HOPE I HAVE BECAUSE I KNOW I WILL SEE MY LOVED ONES AGAIN—THOSE WHO HAVE TRUSTED IN YOU ALONE AS SAVIOR. AMEN.

DON'T WHINE

God is helping you obey Him. . . . Do all things without arguing and talking about how you wish you did not have to do them. In that way, you can prove yourselves to be without blame. You are God's children and no one can talk against you, even in a sin-loving and sin-sick world. You are to shine as lights among the sinful people of this world.

PHILIPPIANS 2:13–15 NLV

How much whining and grumbling have you done lately? We all do it, but it's not fun to admit it. But we *do* need to admit it, and then we need to ask God to help us stop. His Word encourages us to do all things with no whining, complaining, or arguing. When we are positive and full of joy, other people see it and that helps point them to God's goodness and love and salvation. So don't whine. Instead, shine!

HEAVENLY FATHER, PLEASE HELP ME TO SHINE FOR YOU! PLEASE FORGIVE ME AND HELP ME TO SEE WHEN I WHINE TOO MUCH SOMETIMES. I WANT TO DO BETTER AT SHINING LIGHT FOR YOU BY BEING POSITIVE AND FULL OF YOUR JOY NO MATTER WHAT I'M GOING THROUGH. AMEN.

STRENGTH, ROCK, FORTRESS, DELIVERER

I love you, O Lord, my strength. The Lord is my rock and my fortress and my deliverer, my God, my rock, in whom I take refuge, my shield, and the horn of my salvation, my stronghold. I call upon the Lord, who is worthy to be praised, and I am saved from my enemies. . . . In my distress I called upon the Lord; to my God I cried for help. From his temple he heard my voice, and my cry to him reached his ears.

Psalm 18:1–3, 6 ESV

In your quiet time today, focus on God as your strength, your rock, your fortress, your deliverer, and your place of refuge. If you are having trouble in your life—whether it's at school or with friendships or because of stress at home—ask for your heavenly Father's help. Let Him reassure You that He knows what's going on, and He cares about it all. He will help you with any kind of trouble when you depend on Him and His power—and then follow His lead.

ALMIGHTY GOD, THANK YOU FOR BEING MY STRENGTH AND ROCK AND SAFE PLACE. PLEASE HELP ME WITH ANY KIND OF TROUBLE I FIND MYSELF IN. YOU KNOW EVERYTHING, AND NOTHING IS EVER TOO HARD FOR YOU TO HANDLE. I WILL TRUST AND OBEY YOU DURING ANY HARD THING UNTIL YOU RESCUE ME. AMEN.

FOR THOSE WHO LOVE GOD

For those who love God all things work together for good, for those who are called according to his purpose.

ROMANS 8:28 ESV

God's Word promises that He makes everything work together for good for those who love Him. But sometimes that doesn't seem to make sense at all. Like when you prayed for a blessing you never received. Or, worse, you prayed desperately for healing for a loved one, but then that loved one died. It's heartbreaking and confusing.

But just because we're disappointed and hurting and can't understand, that doesn't mean God has changed or His promises aren't true. We must choose to trust Him even more when we can't figure Him out. We must keep faith that His thoughts and ways are much higher than ours (Isaiah 55:8–9) and that He is working in ways we can't currently comprehend. He promises that someday we *will* understand, and so we keep praying to Him, believing Him, and learning from Him.

HEAVENLY FATHER, WHEN I'M HURTING AND CONFUSED, PLEASE KEEP ME EXTRA CLOSE TO YOU, AND SHOW ME YOUR LOVE IN EXTRA SPECIAL WAYS. I DON'T WANT TO TURN AWAY FROM YOU JUST BECAUSE I DON'T UNDERSTAND YOU. AMEN.

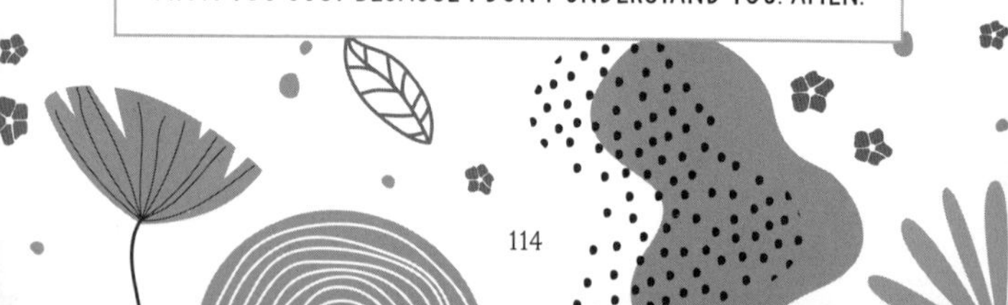

KEEP ON ASKING, SEEKING, KNOCKING

"If you keep knocking long enough, he will get up and give you whatever you need because of your shameless persistence. And so I tell you, keep on asking, and you will receive what you ask for. Keep on seeking, and you will find. Keep on knocking, and the door will be opened to you. For everyone who asks, receives. Everyone who seeks, finds. And to everyone who knocks, the door will be opened."

LUKE 11:8–10 NLT

Do you wonder if God ever gets tired of you coming to Him and asking for things in prayer? Jesus Himself taught in the Bible that God absolutely does not! Do your parents ever get tired of you asking for things? Of course they do! No human parent could ever say they don't get annoyed sometimes by their children's repeated requests. But God is your all-powerful, never-tiring heavenly Father, and in Luke 11 Jesus tells you to keep on asking!

DEAR GOD, THANK YOU FOR NEVER GETTING TIRED OF MY PRAYERS AND SPENDING TIME WITH ME! AMEN.

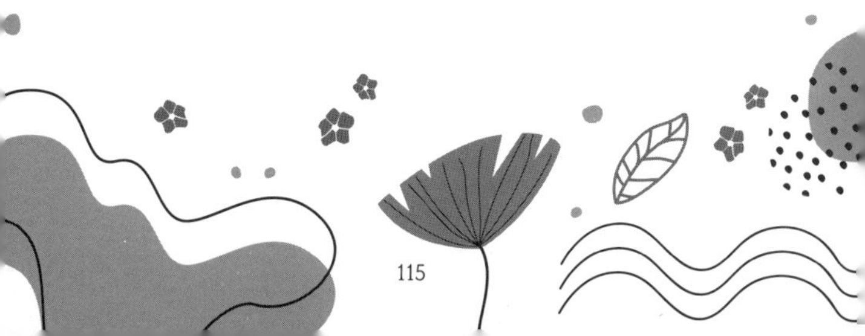

GOD CARES ABOUT EACH OF YOUR TEARS

You keep track of all my sorrows. You have collected all my tears in your bottle. You have recorded each one in your book.

PSALM 56:8 NLT

Through each hard and sad thing in life that makes us cry, we must remember how much God cares about each of our tears and sorrows. The Bible promises He is near when we are brokenhearted, and He heals us (Psalm 34:18; 147:3). He knows and cares about every single one of our sad tears (Psalm 56:8). And for all who believe in Jesus, He is preparing heaven, where "he will wipe every tear from their eyes, and there will be no more death or sorrow or crying or pain. All these things are gone forever" (Revelation 21:4 NLT).

When you are hurting, pray to God and cry to Him. Let Him collect your tears. Focus on the truth of these scriptures. God will help you keep going and help you find joy, and one day He will make everything right.

I'M HURTING, LORD. I NEED YOUR COMFORT, AND I NEED TO REMEMBER THE TRUTH OF YOUR WORD. THANK YOU FOR KEEPING TRACK OF AND CARING ABOUT EVERY TEAR I CRY. AMEN.

WORK WITH ALL YOUR HEART FOR JESUS

Whatever you do, work at it with all your heart, as working for the Lord, not for human masters, since you know that you will receive an inheritance from the Lord as a reward. It is the Lord Christ you are serving.

Colossians 3:23–24 niv

Do you ever get overwhelmed by all your responsibilities in life and school and home? Sometimes you're just tired and bored of it all. Sometimes it feels like it's too much and too hard. Whatever the case, take it all to God. Tell Him how frustrated and overwhelmed you feel. He cares about your feelings and wants to help you.

You can do any job, task, or assignment as if it's praise to God. Do your best at it no matter what it is, saying to God, "Even though this is hard, I want to bring glory and honor to You with the way I work at it and with my attitude in the middle of it." With that kind of attitude in all your work, just watch how God will bless you in His perfect timing.

LORD, PLEASE REMIND ME THAT NO MATTER WHAT I'M WORKING ON, I CAN DO IT IN A WAY THAT BRINGS YOU GLORY—IF I FOCUS MY MIND ON PRAISING AND THANKING YOU ALONG THE WAY. AMEN.

HELP FROM ON HIGH

For the high and honored One Who lives forever, Whose name is Holy, says, "I live in the high and holy place. And I also live with those who are sorry for their sins and have turned from them and are not proud. I give new strength to the spirit of those without pride, and also to those whose hearts are sorry for their sins."

ISAIAH 57:15 NLV

Imagine if you could pick up the phone and call the president of the United States and ask him for help with anything at any time. That role is a pretty big deal, so you would feel confident with the president's power on your side.

Even though not many of us are going to have close connection with important world leaders, it doesn't matter—because we *do* have a close connection and instant communication with the highest King and ultimate world ruler—our one true God who lives in the highest heavens! He promises He is here to help everyone who is humble and sorry for sin and who depends on Him.

ALMIGHTY GOD, YOU ARE THE HIGHEST AND BEST AND MOST POWERFUL OF ALL, AND YET YOU LOVE ME AND WANT TO HELP ME. I AM BEYOND AMAZED AND SO VERY GRATEFUL, AND I LOVE YOU TOO! AMEN.

LOVE BIG, FORGIVE BIG—LIKE JESUS

Above all, love each other deeply,
because love covers over a multitude of sins.

1 PETER 4:8 NIV

You're going to make mistakes in life—probably most days. We all do. And we sure don't want anyone to remember all our mistakes forever. So it's encouraging to know that our mistakes and sins can be covered up by love. Best of all, God's true love covers our sins when we accept Jesus as Savior and believe that the most important act of true love was when He gave Himself up to die on the cross to pay the price for our sin. And when we do our best to love other people like Jesus does and we work on good relationships with our family and friends, then that love helps cover our mistakes we make in those relationships too. Because we love big, we can forgive big—just like Jesus!

DEAR JESUS, THANK YOU FOR COVERING MY MANY SINS AND MISTAKES WITH YOUR BIG LOVE.

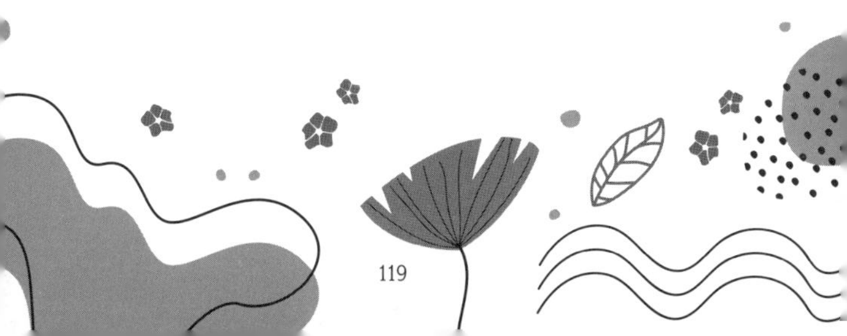

FAMILY DRAMA?

Those who won't care for their relatives, especially those in their own household, have denied the true faith.

1 Timothy 5:8 NLT

Family drama. Can you relate? Of course we won't always get along with our family. The people we love the most often are the ones we spend the most time with, and we're human beings who sin and make mistakes. So it makes sense that we will get on one another's nerves and have fights and conflicts sometimes—maybe even a lot. But when we love big, we can forgive big. And we can promise to give one another grace and always take good care of one another like God tells us to in His Word.

HEAVENLY FATHER, I'M GRATEFUL FOR MY FAMILY. I LOVE THEM SO MUCH. HELP ME TO REMEMBER TO SHOW LOVE AND GRATITUDE EVEN WHEN I'M UPSET WITH THEM. GIVE US YOUR WISDOM WHEN WE'RE IN CONFLICT, PLEASE. HELP US TO WORK THINGS OUT AND FORGIVE ONE ANOTHER AND HAVE PEACE AND JOY AND FUN AGAIN. AMEN.

CHILDREN OF GOD

See what great love the Father has lavished on us, that we should be called children of God! And that is what we are!

1 John 3:1 NIV

When we trust in Jesus Christ as our Savior, we can have a close relationship with God as our heavenly Father. It's so wonderful to have earthly family but even better to know we are in the family of the almighty God.

Sometimes conflicts in earthly families can get big and even scary and unsafe. Maybe that kind of thing has happened in your family, or maybe you've heard about it in a friend's family. So, being part of God's family is especially important because no matter what goes on in earthly families, no matter how broken and troubled they might be, we are always God's children and *no one* can break that family bond. And with the one true God as our loving Father, we have all His care and protection every single day of our lives.

HEAVENLY FATHER, REMIND ME THAT ABOVE ALL YOU ARE MY LOVING HEAVENLY DAD WHO TAKES GOOD CARE OF ME, BOTH NOW AND FOREVER. HELP ME TO SHARE JESUS WITH OTHERS SO THAT MORE PEOPLE CAN BECOME YOUR CHILDREN.

PRAISE GOD FOR THE PRIVILEGE

If you are insulted because you bear the name of Christ, you will be blessed, for the glorious Spirit of God rests upon you. If you suffer, however, it must not be for murder, stealing, making trouble, or prying into other people's affairs. But it is no shame to suffer for being a Christian. Praise God for the privilege of being called by his name!

1 Peter 4:14–16 NLT

You might be mocked and teased for being a Christian, but you don't have to let it bother you. Maybe that sounds impossible, but God's Word says we should not be ashamed; we should be thankful instead.

Being a true Christian means God's Spirit is in us and that we are saved forever. So don't worry about what anyone else says to mock you. Matthew 5:11–12 (NLT) says, "God blesses you when people mock you and persecute you and lie about you and say all sorts of evil things against you because you are my followers. Be happy about it! Be very glad! For a great reward awaits you in heaven."

HELP ME NOT TO BE ANGRY OR ASHAMED WHEN PEOPLE TEASE ME OR ACT MEAN BECAUSE I LOVE AND FOLLOW YOU, JESUS. REMIND ME TO BE HAPPY AND PRAISE YOU BECAUSE YOU HAVE SAVED ME, AND MY REWARD WILL BE GREAT IN HEAVEN. AMEN.

USE YOUR SPECIAL GIFTS

We have different gifts, according to the grace given to each of us. If your gift is prophesying, then prophesy in accordance with your faith; if it is serving, then serve; if it is teaching, then teach; if it is to encourage, then give encouragement; if it is giving, then give generously; if it is to lead, do it diligently; if it is to show mercy, do it cheerfully.

ROMANS 12:6–8 NIV

God has given you special gifts and talents that He wants you to use to help spread His love and bring Him praise! Maybe you have already figured out what some of those gifts are—and you might even discover more gifts as time goes by. Pray for God to help you be sure of the gifts He has given you, and ask Him to show you how to share them in the ways He wants you to.

HEAVENLY FATHER, HELP ME TO KNOW THE SPECIAL GIFTS YOU'VE CREATED WITHIN ME. SHOW ME HOW YOU WANT ME TO USE THEM. HELP ME TO POINT MANY PEOPLE TOWARD KNOWING AND LOVING YOU! AMEN.

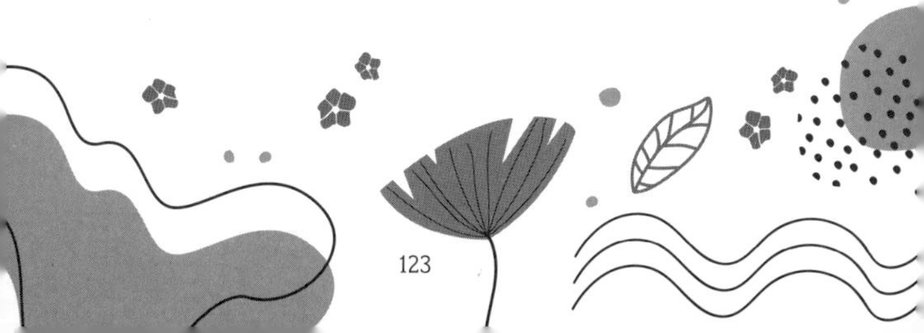

ARE YOU HEAVY LADEN?

"Come to me, all who labor and are heavy laden, and I will give you rest. Take my yoke upon you, and learn from me, for I am gentle and lowly in heart, and you will find rest for your souls. For my yoke is easy, and my burden is light."

MATTHEW 11:28–30 ESV

What feels heavy in your life today? Maybe it's a ton of schoolwork or drama among your friends. Maybe you're fighting with someone in your family. Maybe it's a broken heart. Whatever it is, Jesus says to bring it to Him and He will help you with it. He will give you a break from it and help you feel peaceful and rested. Ask Him what to do about your heavy load, and then listen and let Him teach you through prayer, worship, and His Word.

DEAR JESUS, PLEASE HELP ME TO HAVE A BREAK FROM MY PROBLEMS AND PAIN. I NEED YOUR REST, PEACE, AND COMFORT. PLEASE GUIDE ME AND SHOW ME HOW TO DEAL WITH THE HARD THINGS GOING ON IN MY LIFE THE WAY YOU WANT ME TO. AMEN.

HEROES OF THE FAITH

Faith shows the reality of what we hope for; it is the evidence of things we cannot see. Through their faith, the people in days of old earned a good reputation.

HEBREWS 11:1–2 NLT

In your quiet time today, think about your family and friends—those who are still living and those who have passed away—who have super strong faith in God. You can gain wisdom and encouragement by learning from them.

Hebrews chapter 11 is a wonderful passage of scripture to help us remember a whole list of great faith heroes of Bible times—people like Noah, Moses, Joseph, Sarah, and Rahab, who continued to believe in God and His promises even during the worst of times in their lives. Like them, we should want to hold on to our faith no matter what. Spend time reading more about these heroes of the faith and follow their examples.

DEAR GOD, PLEASE HELP ME TO REMEMBER EVERYONE WHO HAS GONE BEFORE ME WHO KEPT GREAT FAITH IN YOU. I WANT TO BE STRONG IN MY FAITH TOO. AMEN.

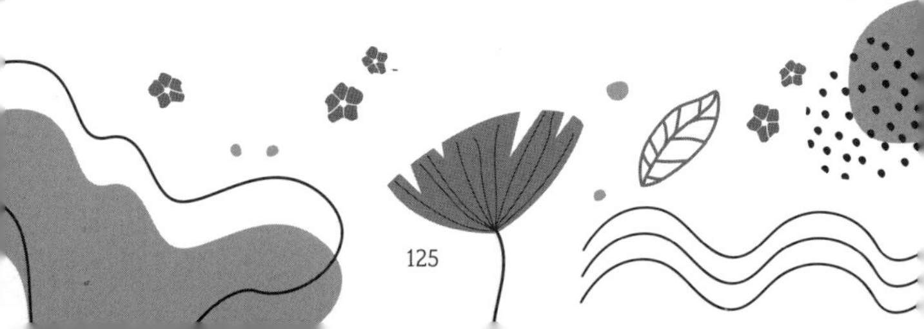

THE FATHER'S GOOD GIFTS

"You parents—if your children ask for a loaf of bread, do you give them a stone instead? Or if they ask for a fish, do you give them a snake? Of course not! So if you sinful people know how to give good gifts to your children, how much more will your heavenly Father give good gifts to those who ask him."

Matthew 7:9–11 NLT

God loves to bless you and give you good gifts, so pray in big ways and ask Him for the things you need and want. Never stop praying to Him and telling Him why you need or want those things. As you draw closer to Him, He will bless you—not always exactly in the ways you hoped or wanted but always in ways you never dreamed of and that are best for you.

HEAVENLY FATHER, THANK YOU FOR WANTING TO GIVE ME GOOD THINGS. I COME TO YOU AND ASK YOU FOR THESE THINGS I NEED AND WANT: ________________. BUT PLEASE CHANGE MY MIND ABOUT MY WANTS AND NEEDS IF THEY DON'T MATCH YOUR PLANS FOR ME. I TRUST MY LIFE TO YOU, AND I TRUST YOU TO BLESS ME IN THE WAYS YOU KNOW ARE BEST. AMEN.

HAPPINESS VS. JOY, PART 1

Being with You is to be full of joy.
In Your right hand there is happiness forever.
PSALM 16:11 NLV

"Whatever makes you happy!" It may be a popular saying, but it's one we need to be careful with because if our constant goal is just to be happy, we can truly ruin our lives. Think of it this way: Lots of people would be happy to be on vacation every single day, right? But how would they earn money to live? Vacation can make us all really happy, but it has to be balanced wisely with time for work and learning and other needs of life. That's why joy is so much more important than happiness.

Real joy is based on relationship with Jesus and hope of perfect heaven with Him forever, while happiness is usually just based on whatever situation we're in. When we focus on real joy and apply it to everything we do, that's when we can also find happiness in pretty much anything!

DEAR GOD, HELP ME TO KEEP LEARNING ABOUT HOW REAL JOY IN YOU IS FAR BETTER THAN JUST HAPPINESS. AMEN.

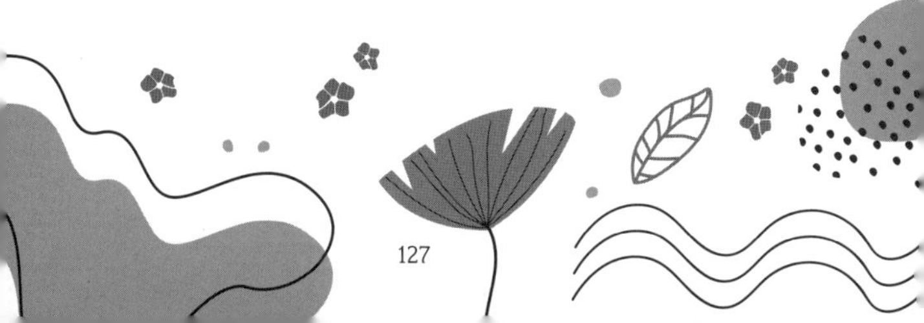

HAPPINESS VS. JOY, PART 2

"The joy of the LORD is your strength."

NEHEMIAH 8:10 NIV

Our feelings can change quickly and easily. Something that made you happy last year or even a month ago might seem ridiculous to you now. That's another example of how real joy is so much better than happiness. Focus on these scriptures in your quiet time today to help teach you about knowing real joy:

- "I have placed the Lord always in front of me. Because He is at my right hand, I will not be moved. And so my heart is glad. My soul is full of joy" (Psalm 16:8–9 NLV).
- "You have never seen Him but you love Him. You cannot see Him now but you are putting your trust in Him. And you have joy so great that words cannot tell about it. You will get what your faith is looking for, which is to be saved from the punishment of sin" (1 Peter 1:8–9 NLV).

DEAR GOD, NO MATTER WHAT EMOTIONS I'M FEELING, HELP ME TO REMEMBER THAT TRUE JOY IS ALWAYS FOUND IN YOU.

LIGHT SO BRIGHT

At the right time, we will be shown that God is the One Who has all power. He is the King of kings and Lord of lords. He can never die. He lives in a light so bright that no man can go near Him. No man has ever seen God or can see Him. Honor and power belong to Him forever.

1 Timothy 6:15–16 NLV

No one yet has ever fully seen God because He is so awesome that we humans just aren't able to look at Him. It's kind of like trying to look at the sun. We know the sun is there, and we can see it and all the good it does. But it's not possible for our human eyes to look at it directly because it's just too much! Our eyes were not made to look at something so bright. But someday, at just the right time, the Bible tells us, we will get to see God fully, and we will see how awesome and powerful He is over everything in all creation.

ALMIGHTY GOD, EVEN THOUGH I CAN'T FULLY SEE YOU RIGHT NOW, I TRUST THAT YOU ARE WORKING AND GUIDING ME. IT'S AMAZING TO KNOW THAT ONE DAY I WILL SEE YOU FULLY! AMEN.

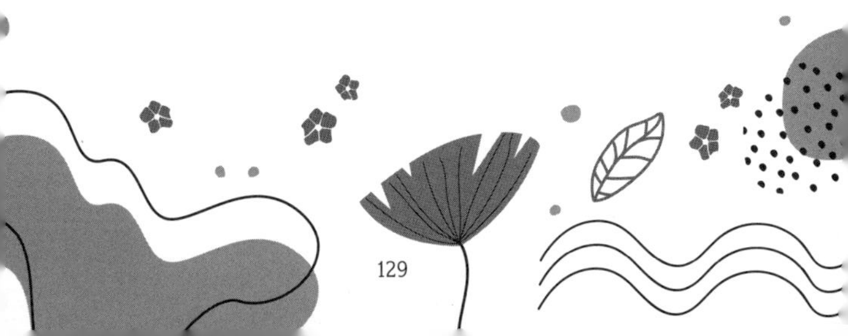

YOU ARE FREE!

Be careful that you do not please your old selves by sinning because you are free. Live this free life by loving and helping others.

GALATIANS 5:13 NLV

Faith in Jesus Christ brings freedom—the very best kind of freedom: freedom from sin. And no one can *ever* take that freedom from you.

Jesus paid the price for sin, and when we trust in Him as Savior, He removes it from us. That doesn't mean that we won't ever make bad choices again and suffer the consequences in this life, but Jesus takes away the forever punishment for those bad choices. He also helps us admit sins and want to get rid of them when we do make bad choices.

While, yes, we do have freedom from sin, we should never want to play around with sin. Instead, we should always want to use our freedom from sin to love and serve others.

DEAR JESUS, THANK YOU THAT I HAVE THE BEST KIND OF FREEDOM BECAUSE YOU DIED ON THE CROSS TO TAKE THE PUNISHMENT AND PAY THE PRICE FOR MY SIN. THEN YOU ROSE TO LIFE AGAIN, AND YOU GIVE ME FOREVER LIFE TOO. IT'S AMAZING! HELP ME TO USE MY FREEDOM TO TRULY LOVE AND HELP OTHERS. AMEN.

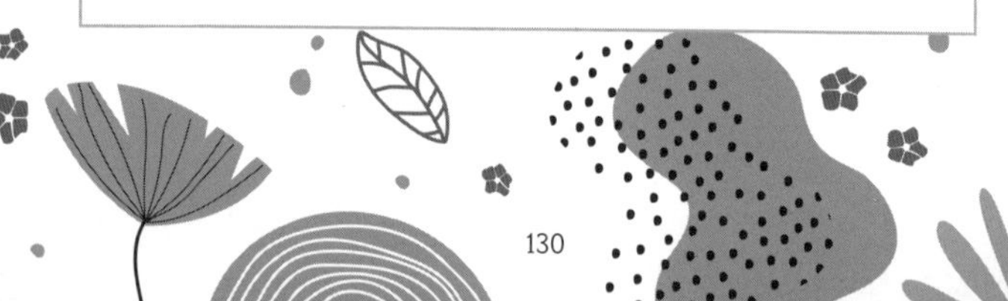

WORDS HAVE POWER, PART 1

We can make a large horse go wherever we want by means of a small bit in its mouth. And a small rudder makes a huge ship turn wherever the pilot chooses to go, even though the winds are strong. In the same way, the tongue is a small thing that makes grand speeches. But a tiny spark can set a great forest on fire. And among all the parts of the body, the tongue is a flame of fire. It is a whole world of wickedness, corrupting your entire body. It can set your whole life on fire, for it is set on fire by hell itself. People can tame all kinds of animals, birds, reptiles, and fish, but no one can tame the tongue.

JAMES 3:3–8 NLT

The words we speak matter. They hold a lot of power. So, we must remember that God says we need to watch our words and be careful with them. Proverbs 21:23 (NLT) says, "Watch your tongue and keep your mouth shut, and you will stay out of trouble." And Ephesians 4:29 (NLT) says, "Don't use foul or abusive language. Let everything you say be good and helpful, so that your words will be an encouragement to those who hear them."

LORD, PLEASE HELP ME TO REMEMBER THAT THE WORDS I SAY MATTER AND THAT THEY ARE POWERFUL. PLEASE HELP ME TO USE MY MOUTH AND TONGUE WISELY. AMEN.

WORDS HAVE POWER, PART 2

If a person thinks he is religious, but does not keep his tongue from speaking bad things, he is fooling himself. His religion is worth nothing.

James 1:26 NLV

If we say we love and follow Jesus as our Savior, then we also need to care a lot about what we say and the power of our words. And if we mess up and lie or say bad things, we need to confess and apologize and correct that sin as quickly as possible. Here are more scriptures to help us:

- "A gentle answer turns away anger, but a sharp word causes anger. The tongue of the wise uses much learning in a good way, but the mouth of fools speaks in a foolish way" (Proverbs 15:1–2 NLV).
- "Too much talk leads to sin. Be sensible and keep your mouth shut" (Proverbs 10:19 NLT).
- "If you want to enjoy life and see many happy days, keep your tongue from speaking evil and your lips from telling lies" (1 Peter 3:10 NLT).

DEAR GOD, PLEASE "PUT A WATCH OVER MY MOUTH. KEEP WATCH OVER THE DOOR OF MY LIPS" (PSALM 141:3 NLV). THANK YOU! AMEN.

DRAW NEAR TO GOD

Draw near to God, and he will draw near to you.

JAMES 4:8 ESV

Since the Bible says God already knows everything you're going to say before you even say it (Psalm 139:4; Matthew 6:8), you might wonder why it matters whether you spend quiet time with God and pray to Him. Maybe you have a family member or best friend you are so close to who can almost seem to read your mind like God can. If your friend knows you that well, then why do you care about spending time with her? Because you love her and enjoy being together and doing things together, right? In the same way, God wants to be your absolute best, *best* friend. He loves you and knows you more than any person ever possibly could, and He hopes you will want to spend time with Him and be a part of all the good things He is doing.

DEAR GOD, I CHOOSE QUIET TIME WITH YOU BECAUSE I LOVE YOU AND WANT TO LEARN MORE ABOUT YOU. I LOOK FORWARD TO SPENDING TIME WITH YOU AS MY VERY BEST FRIEND OF ALL. AMEN.

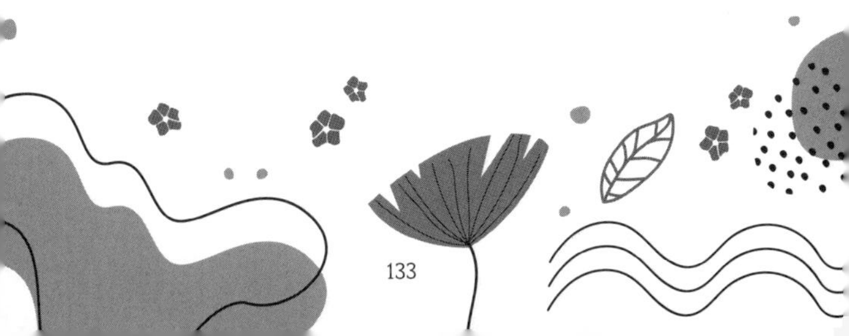

THE STRONGEST KIND OF STRENGTH

[The Lord] said to me, "My grace is sufficient for you, for my power is made perfect in weakness." Therefore I will boast all the more gladly about my weaknesses, so that Christ's power may rest on me. That is why, for Christ's sake, I delight in weaknesses, in insults, in hardships, in persecutions, in difficulties. For when I am weak, then I am strong.

2 Corinthians 12:9–10 NIV

God doesn't want us to be strong on our own—that's not because He's mean and selfish and on a power trip. It's because He wants us to be truly strong with the most powerful, best kind of strength. We are strong because we are full of *His* power, not our own. God doesn't just want good things for us, He wants the *very best* things for us—and the best things are always found in Him!

ALMIGHTY GOD, HELP ME TO BE HAPPY TO BE WEAK ON MY OWN. I'M ONLY TRULY STRONG WHEN I'M DEPENDING ON YOU FOR EVERYTHING. THANK YOU! AMEN.

WITHOUT EXCUSE

What may be known about God is plain to them, because God has made it plain to them. For since the creation of the world God's invisible qualities—his eternal power and divine nature—have been clearly seen, being understood from what has been made, so that people are without excuse.

ROMANS 1:19–20 NIV

Do you know that every person can know about God by simply looking around outside in nature? God has shown Himself through everything He has made. Anyone can know that God is real by observing all the cool details in animals, plants, mountains, forests, and seas. Anyone can see Him in the remarkable ways our bodies are designed and the ways animals know how to hunt for their food or build themselves homes. Our Creator God is awesome, and He deserves all our worship and praise!

I LOVE SEEING YOUR WORK IN ALL THE THINGS YOU HAVE MADE, LORD! THANK YOU FOR MAKING YOURSELF KNOWN THROUGH YOUR AMAZING CREATION! I PRAY THAT MORE PEOPLE WOULD ALSO KNOW JESUS AS SAVIOR. AMEN.

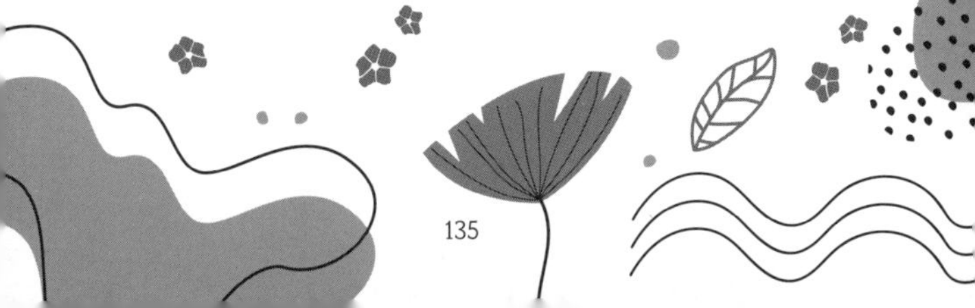

BE FULL OF JOY AND PEACE

Be full of joy always because you belong to the Lord. Again I say, be full of joy! . . . Do not worry. Learn to pray about everything. Give thanks to God as you ask Him for what you need. The peace of God is much greater than the human mind can understand. This peace will keep your hearts and minds through Christ Jesus.

PHILIPPIANS 4:4, 6–7 NLV

You have every reason to be full of joy right now no matter what hard or sad thing is going on in your day, your month, your year, your life. You can be full of joy because you belong to God—if you have asked Jesus to be your Savior, that is. You have nothing to worry about and everything to pray about. And, as you trust in God and communicate with Him through prayer with thanks for who He is and all He does, you will have peace and joy that no one can explain, because the one true God is crazy amazing!

DEAR LORD, I BELIEVE THAT YOU TAKE MY WORRIES AND TROUBLES AND YOU REPLACE THEM WITH UNFAILING PEACE AND JOY. I'M SO GRATEFUL THAT BECAUSE OF JESUS I BELONG TO YOU. AMEN.

ADD TO YOUR FAITH

For this very reason, make every effort to add to your faith goodness; and to goodness, knowledge; and to knowledge, self-control; and to self-control, perseverance; and to perseverance, godliness; and to godliness, mutual affection; and to mutual affection, love. For if you possess these qualities in increasing measure, they will keep you from being ineffective and unproductive in your knowledge of our Lord Jesus Christ.

2 Peter 1:5–8 NIV

You might be very sociable and outgoing, or you might be on the quieter side. Both personalities are wonderful! What matters is that you're aware of how God made you to be and that you ask Him to help you use the personality and gifts He's given you to serve Him. God can grow and develop you with new traits, gifts, and skills according to His will, so let Him! But to accomplish all these things, you need to stay in constant good relationship and communication with Him. So never stop praying. Never stop reading God's Word. Never stop learning from and serving your loving heavenly Father.

DEAR GOD, PLEASE HELP ME TO LEARN MORE ABOUT MYSELF AND HOW YOU DESIGNED ME. I WANT TO KEEP LEARNING FROM YOU AND STAYING CLOSE TO YOU. AMEN.

GIVE, BECAUSE GOD HAS GIVEN TO YOU

You will be enriched in every way so that you can always be generous. And when we take your gifts to those who need them, they will thank God. So two good things will result from this ministry of giving—the needs of the believers in Jerusalem will be met, and they will joyfully express their thanks to God. As a result of your ministry, they will give glory to God. For your generosity to them and to all believers will prove that you are obedient to the Good News of Christ. And they will pray for you with deep affection because of the overflowing grace God has given to you. Thank God for this gift too wonderful for words!

2 Corinthians 9:11–15 NLT

Every good thing you have came from God, and He wants you to share those gifts and blessings. Share them with others, whether that's giving money or food to people in need, serving at church, or sharing your talents with others. This spreads God's love and helps more and more people come to trust in Jesus as Savior.

DEAR JESUS, YOU ARE THE GREATEST GIFT. YOU HAVE GIVEN ME ALL MY GIFTS AND BLESSINGS. I WANT TO SHARE THEM WITH OTHERS SO THAT THEY CAN KNOW YOU AS SAVIOR TOO. AMEN.

WATCH YOUR ATTITUDE

Be happy in your hope. Do not give up when trouble comes. Do not let anything stop you from praying.

ROMANS 12:12 NLV

Is there anything that has you feeling depressed today? It's no wonder, since there are all kinds of hard and sad things in life that disappoint and depress us. We can easily feel sad and gloomy. So we sometimes must make a choice to be positive anyway, and God's Word can help us.

Romans 12:12 tells us that even if what's going on in our lives isn't happy, we can be happy in our hope in Jesus. We can choose never to give up, even when troubles come. And we can keep on praying no matter what because God never leaves us and He always wants us to talk to Him and ask for His help.

DEAR JESUS, PLEASE HELP ME TO WATCH MY ATTITUDE. HELP ME TO HAVE A HAPPY-IN-HOPE, NEVER-GIVE-UP, ALWAYS-PRAYING-TO-YOU KIND OF OUTLOOK. I CAN ONLY DO THIS WITH YOUR HELP. AMEN.

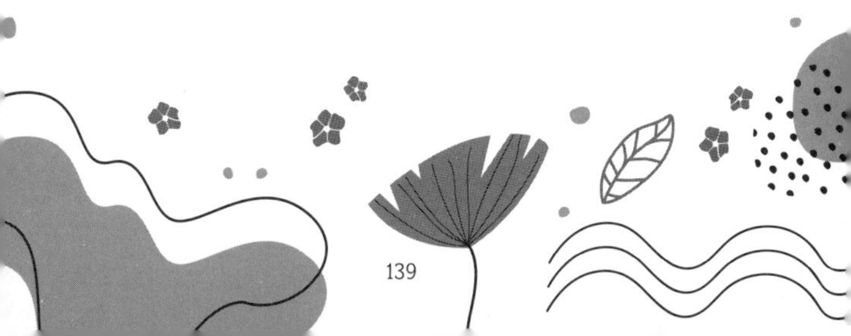

THE LORD WILL FIGHT FOR YOU

And Moses said to the people, "Fear not, stand firm, and see the salvation of the Lord, *which he will work for you today. For the Egyptians whom you see today, you shall never see again. The* Lord *will fight for you, and you have only to be silent."*

Exodus 14:13–14 ESV

Throughout the Bible, there are many times God worked in miraculous, against-all-odds ways to save and help His people. In your quiet time today, read more of the stories of Moses and the Israelites and focus on how God can help with any problem you have, no matter how big and horrible it seems. He will fight for you. Just wait and see how He will save you. Keep coming to Him for help and peace.

ALMIGHTY GOD, YOU KNOW EXACTLY WHAT I'M GOING THROUGH WITH ANY PROBLEM OR ENEMY I FACE. YOU KNOW MY FEARS AND WORRIES. YOU KNOW HOW TO SOLVE ALL THE PROBLEMS AND DEFEAT ANY ENEMIES. HELP ME TO BE STILL AND STRONG AS I PRAY TO YOU. I'M DEPENDING ON YOU! I BELIEVE YOU WILL DO THE FIGHTING FOR ME AND WILL COME TO MY RESCUE. AMEN.

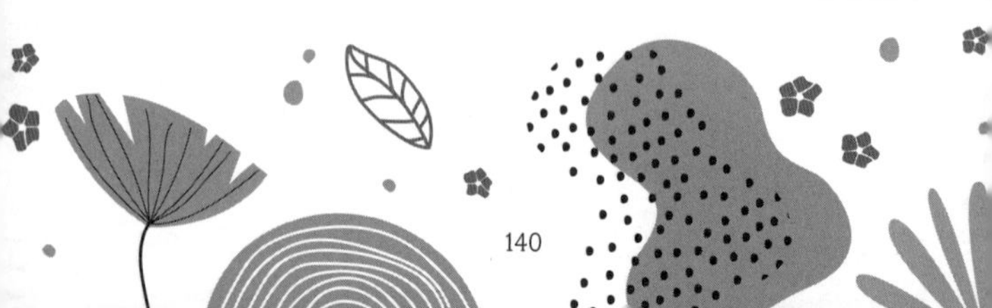

TRUE KINDNESS, PART 1

Your kindness will reward you, but your cruelty will destroy you.

PROVERBS 11:17 NLT

Have you ever had to deal with mean girls? It's awful, isn't it? Maybe you've messed up and acted like a mean girl yourself. If you have, then you need to admit your sin, apologize, and make it right with the people you hurt—and then do better at being truly kind. God loves and forgives you!

We all sin and act unkind sometimes, and so we need to focus on God's Word to help us:

- "As we have opportunity, let us do good to everyone, and especially to those who are of the household of faith" (Galatians 6:10 ESV).
- "We know what real love is because Jesus gave up his life for us. So we also ought to give up our lives for our brothers and sisters. . . . Dear children, let's not merely say that we love each other; let us show the truth by our actions" (1 John 3:16, 18 NLT).

DEAR GOD, HELP ME TO REMEMBER THAT BEING KIND IS REWARDING. HELP ME NEVER TO WANT TO BE MEAN TO OTHERS AND TO BE SINCERELY SORRY IF I AM MEAN SOMETIMES. PLEASE FILL ME WITH YOUR TRUE KINDNESS TO SHARE WITH OTHERS. AMEN.

TRUE KINDNESS, PART 2

Love is patient and kind.

1 Corinthians 13:4 ESV

Being kind to others doesn't mean you have to be close friends with every person around you. That's not even possible. And if you tried, you'd never have time for everyone and for the good things God has planned for you. And being kind to others doesn't mean you must agree about everything. You can agree to disagree and still show kindness and respect.

When you remember that every single person in the world (no matter who they are or what they do or what their personality is like) is created and loved by God, He helps you to be truly kind and respectful to anyone who comes into your life.

DEAR GOD, PLEASE HELP ME TO REMEMBER THAT ALL PEOPLE ARE MADE IN YOUR IMAGE AND ARE LOVED BY YOU. HELP ME TO TREAT EVERYONE KINDLY AND RESPECTFULLY WHILE ALSO HAVING WISDOM FROM YOUR WORD ABOUT FRIENDSHIP AND KNOWING MY LIMITS. AMEN.

BE CAREFUL WITH COMPARISON

We brought nothing into the world, and we cannot take anything out of the world. But if we have food and clothing, with these we will be content. But those who desire to be rich fall into temptation, into a snare, into many senseless and harmful desires that plunge people into ruin and destruction. For the love of money is a root of all kinds of evils.

1 Timothy 6:7–10 ESV

Be careful with comparing! It's easy to get caught up in feeling like what we have in our lives is less than what social media and television say we should have. We all need help from God to be content with simple things in this life. If we have what we truly need, we should be grateful and happy, and all other things are just extra blessings on top that we shouldn't always expect or feel entitled to.

DEAR GOD, PLEASE HELP ME TO BE HAPPY AND SATISFIED WITH JUST THE THINGS I NEED. HELP ME NOT TO FEEL ENTITLED TO MORE THAN THAT—THOUGH YOU ALSO BLESS ME WITH MANY EXTRAS. I'M GRATEFUL FOR ALL YOUR GOODNESS. AMEN.

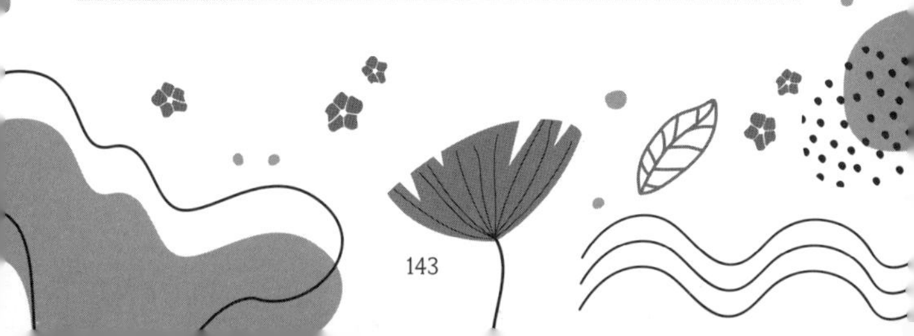

PRAY FOR OUR NATION AND GOVERNMENT

Pray for kings and all others who are in power over us so we might live quiet God-like lives in peace. It is good when you pray like this. It pleases God Who is the One Who saves.

1 Timothy 2:2–3 NLV

Pray for our nation and government in your quiet time today. It can be confusing and overwhelming to understand everything that is going on. But there is always something you can do to help: you can pray, of course! The American flag can be your reminder. Every time you see it, pray something like this:

> PLEASE BLESS OUR NATION ACCORDING TO YOUR WILL, GOD. HELP OUR LEADERS HAVE A DESIRE TO HONOR YOU. PLEASE GIVE THEM YOUR WISDOM TO GOVERN WELL. MAY EACH OF THEM KNOW YOU AS THE ONE TRUE GOD AND SAVIOR. PLEASE PROTECT OUR NATION AND OUR FREEDOM TO WORSHIP YOU, AND HELP US TO USE THAT FREEDOM TO SPREAD YOUR TRUTH AND LOVE. AMEN.

PRAY FOR THE WHOLE WORLD

"Be still, and know that I am God! I will be honored by every nation. I will be honored throughout the world."

PSALM 46:10 NLT

In addition to praying for our country and our government, you can pray specifically for each state too. Don't just stop there. God loves *everyone everywhere* in the whole world, not just our nation. So start praying for every person in every country and for all nations to honor the one true God and to do His will according to His Word.

DEAR GOD, YOU LOVE ALL PEOPLE OF ALL NATIONS. YOU WANT THEM TO HONOR YOU AND TRUST JESUS AS SAVIOR SO THAT YOU CAN GIVE THEM ETERNAL LIFE. YOU ARE SUCH A GOOD AND LOVING HEAVENLY FATHER. HELP ME TO REMEMBER TO PRAY FOR ALL PEOPLE EVERYWHERE! AMEN.

LET THE TEARS FLOW

Then Jesus cried.

John 11:35 NLV

Could you use a good cry today? It's okay if you do! Let the tears flow in your quiet time. Sometimes crying is because of frustration and sadness. Maybe you just need time and space to feel those emotions and give them to God in prayer.

If we hold in our emotions, they often explode in other, not-so-good ways, or they can even make us feel sick inside. So don't ever think that crying means you're not strong. Listening to and figuring out where your emotions are coming from and then giving them time and space to release takes a lot of maturity and courage. When you can name your emotions and realize the source of them, they won't scare you or cause you to act out in ways that might get you in trouble. Sharing your emotions with God and mature people who care all about you is one of the very best ways to deal with your feelings.

I'M SO GLAD I CAN CRY TO YOU, LORD, AND THAT YOU ALWAYS CARE. HELP ME TO LISTEN TO MY EMOTIONS AND FIGURE OUT HOW TO HANDLE THEM IN HEALTHY WAYS, USING YOUR WISDOM. AMEN.

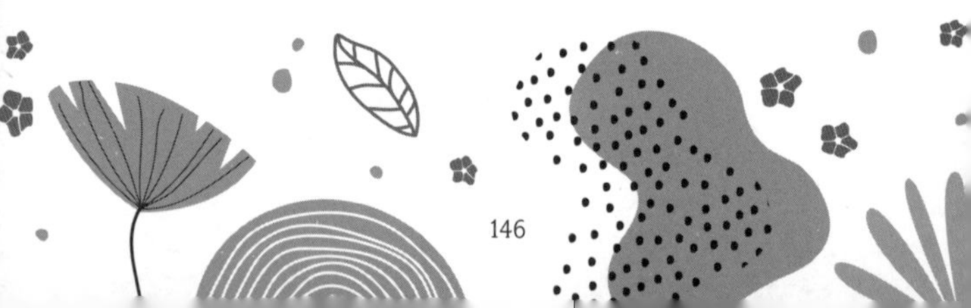

GOD IS NOT SLOW

Do not forget this one thing, dear friends:
With the Lord a day is like a thousand years, and a thousand years are like a day. The Lord is not slow in keeping his promise, as some understand slowness. Instead he is patient with you, not wanting anyone to perish, but everyone to come to repentance.

2 PETER 3:8–9 NIV

God is far beyond what our brains can understand—including the way He views time. We need to be patient, even when it seems like He isn't keeping His promises. God is not being slow or ignoring us. His main goal is to save as many people as possible from their sins and give them eternal life in paradise, and He is doing everything with His perfect plans. We can trust Him.

I'M SORRY I HAVE SO MUCH TROUBLE WAITING ON YOU SOMETIMES, LORD. PLEASE REMIND ME HOW MUCH YOU LOVE ALL PEOPLE AND HOW PERFECT YOUR PLANS AND TIMING ALWAYS ARE. AMEN.

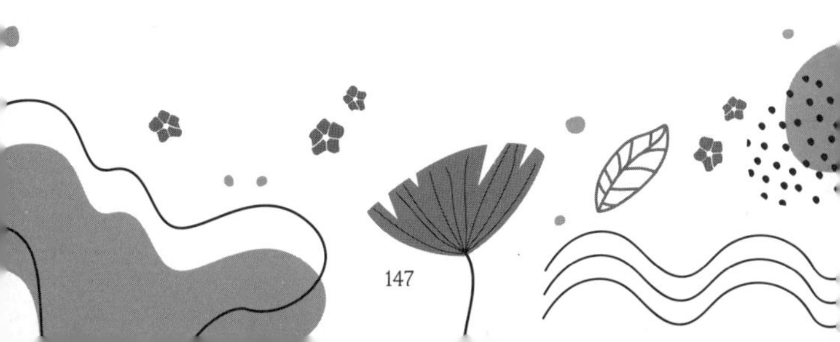

BE A HUMBLE SERVANT LIKE JESUS

When [Jesus] had finished washing their feet, he put on his clothes and returned to his place. "Do you understand what I have done for you?" he asked them. "You call me 'Teacher' and 'Lord,' and rightly so, for that is what I am. Now that I, your Lord and Teacher, have washed your feet, you also should wash one another's feet. I have set you an example that you should do as I have done for you. Very truly I tell you, no servant is greater than his master, nor is a messenger greater than the one who sent him. Now that you know these things, you will be blessed if you do them."

John 13:12–17 NIV

Jesus is King of kings and Lord of lords. Even the winds and the waves obey Him (Matthew 8:27). Everyone on earth will one day bow before Him. And yet He is truly a humble servant leader. He demonstrated that by even washing His disciples' feet. And He instructed them that they should do likewise and they would be blessed for being humble, obedient servants of one another. That message was not just for the disciples—it's for us today too.

JESUS, THANK YOU FOR SHOWING US HUMILITY, COMPASSION, SERVICE, AND LOVE. I WANT TO BE LIKE YOU AND TREAT OTHERS LIKE YOU DO. AMEN.

READY FOR THE BEST

In a wealthy home some utensils are made of gold and silver, and some are made of wood and clay. The expensive utensils are used for special occasions, and the cheap ones are for everyday use. If you keep yourself pure, you will be a special utensil for honorable use. Your life will be clean, and you will be ready for the Master to use you for every good work. Run from anything that stimulates youthful lusts. Instead, pursue righteous living, faithfulness, love, and peace. Enjoy the companionship of those who call on the Lord with pure hearts.

2 Timothy 2:20–22 NLT

In your quiet time today, focus on this scripture from 2 Timothy and how you want God to use your life. Do you want to be just like regular, everyday wood and clay, or do you want to be like shining gold used for the most special purposes? When you work hard to live a clean life, as far away from sin as possible, God can use you for the very best things He has planned.

PLEASE KEEP SHOWING ME WHAT AREAS OF MY LIFE NEED TO BE CLEANED UP, LORD. HELP ME TO STAY FAR AWAY FROM THINGS THAT ARE BAD FOR ME. ALIGN MY LIFE WITH THE WONDERFUL PLAN YOU HAVE FOR ME. AMEN.

JESUS IS COMING BACK AGAIN

The Spirit teaches you everything you need to know, and what he teaches is true—it is not a lie. So just as he has taught you, remain in fellowship with Christ. And now, dear children, remain in fellowship with Christ so that when he returns, you will be full of courage and not shrink back from him in shame.

1 John 2:27–28 NLT

As Christians, we're supposed to be ready for Jesus to return to earth at any moment (Matthew 24:44; Luke 12:40). For some people, that might sound ridiculous or scary, but for those of us who stay close to Jesus, it should be exciting! It should fill us with the best kind of joy and hope! If we remain in fellowship with Jesus, we will be full of courage and not shrink back with fear or be ashamed in any way when Jesus returns to earth.

DEAR JESUS, I BELIEVE YOU WILL COME BACK AGAIN RIGHT ON TIME ACCORDING TO YOUR PERFECT SCHEDULE. PLEASE KEEP ME CLOSE TO YOU. HELP ME TO MAKE GOOD HABITS OF SPENDING TIME WITH YOU AND TO WANT MORE AND MORE GOOD FELLOWSHIP WITH YOU. AMEN.

BROKEN AND IMPERFECT

Now that which we see is as if we were looking in a broken mirror. But then we will see everything. Now I know only a part. But then I will know everything in a perfect way. That is how God knows me right now.

1 Corinthians 13:12 NLV

When you're praying in your quiet time and asking God for answers but not understanding His ways, this verse is an important one to remember. Everything in this world is not the perfect way God intended it because sin entered the world when Adam and Eve chose to disobey God. And the way we see and try to understand is broken and imperfect too because of sin. But God is working out His plans, and at just the right time He will make all things new and right. Then we will see things perfectly as He does, and that will be amazing!

DEAR GOD, HELP ME TO TRUST YOU EVEN WHEN I'M CONFUSED AND HURTING. PLEASE GIVE ME PEACE THAT AT JUST THE RIGHT TIME YOU WILL MAKE EVERYTHING TURN OUT RIGHT AND GOOD FOREVER. AMEN.

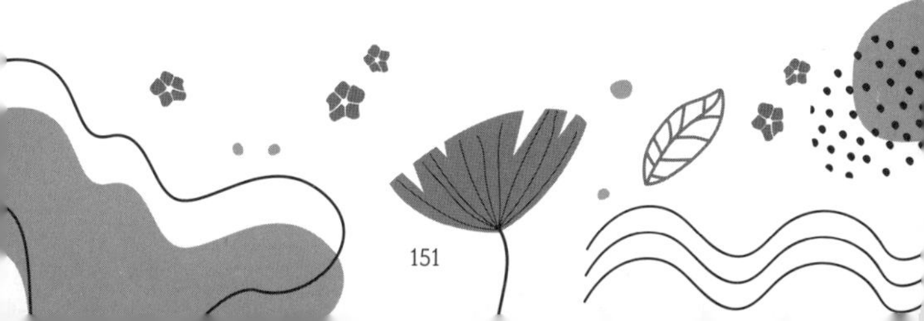

GOD CAN STRENGTHEN YOUR FAITH

"Lord, I have faith. Help my weak faith to be stronger!"

MARK 9:24 NLV

If you're ever struggling to understand what God is doing or not doing about your prayer requests, it's good to remember this story from the Bible. A father was asking Jesus for help for his son, and it was hard for the man to imagine that Jesus could do what he was asking. The father said to Jesus,

> "Have mercy on us and help us, if you can."
>
> "What do you mean, 'If I can'?" Jesus asked. Anything is possible if a person believes."
>
> The father instantly cried out, "I do believe, but help me overcome my unbelief!" (Mark 9:22–24 NLT)

When we pray, we have to remember that God is able to do exactly what we ask—but also so much more! He may or may not answer the way we hope, but no matter how He responds to our prayers, our main response to God should be, "Lord, I have faith. Help my weak faith to be stronger!"

PLEASE MAKE MY FAITH STRONGER AND STRONGER EACH DAY, LORD! I BELIEVE ANYTHING IS POSSIBLE WITH YOU! THANK YOU FOR HEARING MY PRAYERS. AMEN.

KNOW THAT HE IS GOD!

God is our refuge and strength, always ready to help in times of trouble. So we will not fear when earthquakes come and the mountains crumble into the sea. Let the oceans roar and foam. Let the mountains tremble as the waters surge! . . . God's voice thunders, and the earth melts! The Lord of Heaven's Armies is here among us; the God of Israel is our fortress. Come, see the glorious works of the Lord. . . . "Be still, and know that I am God! I will be honored by every nation. I will be honored throughout the world." The Lord of Heaven's Armies is here among us; the God of Israel is our fortress.

Psalm 46:1–3, 6–8, 10–11 NLT

How often do you stop to think about God's awesome greatness and power? Right now, in your quiet time, be still and think about how nothing is mightier than God. Nothing is ever beyond His control. He cares about every detail of your life, no matter how big or small. He is your strength and safe place no matter where you are or what you're going through.

RIGHT NOW I JUST WANT TO SIT AND THINK ABOUT HOW AWESOME YOU ARE, LORD. I PRAISE YOU, AND I'M GRATEFUL FOR YOU! AMEN.

ARE YOU EASYGOING?

Get rid of all bitterness, rage and anger, brawling and slander, along with every form of malice. Be kind and compassionate to one another, forgiving each other, just as in Christ God forgave you.

EPHESIANS 4:31–32 NIV

Would you call yourself easygoing or not? Do you get angry easily when plans you were looking forward to end up changing? Maybe your family had to cancel vacation because of illness or there was no money for the private lessons you wanted because of a job loss in your family. Of course, you'll feel sad or upset about those kinds of things—but you can choose to hold on to anger and a bad mood, or you can choose to be easygoing, forgiving, understanding, and loving when your family is going through a hard time or when your plans get ruined. Anger and poor attitudes will just make a bad situation worse, but being easygoing, understanding, and loving will bless you and everyone around you.

DEAR GOD, WHEN I'M UPSET THAT PLANS HAD TO CHANGE, PLEASE HELP ME TO CHOOSE A GOOD ATTITUDE WITH FORGIVENESS, UNDERSTANDING, AND LOVE. AMEN.

OBEY AND BE BLESSED

"Be faithful in obeying the Lord your God. Be careful to keep all His Laws which I tell you today. And the Lord your God will set you high above all the nations of the earth. All these good things will come upon you if you will obey the Lord your God. Good will come to you in the city, and good will come to you in the country. Good will come to your children, and the fruit of your ground, and the young of your animals. Your cattle and flock will have many young ones. Good will come to your basket and your bread pan. Good will come to you when you come in, and when you go out."

DEUTERONOMY 28:1–6 NLV

God made it very clear in His Word that if His people obey Him, He will bless us in every area of our lives. And who can bless better than the one true God who created everything and is the giver of every good gift?

I WANT TO OBEY YOU BECAUSE I LOVE YOU, LORD! I TRUST THAT YOU WILL BLESS ME AND BRING GOOD TO ME IN MANY WAYS WHEN I FOLLOW YOU. YOU HAVE PROMISED THAT, AND YOU ALWAYS KEEP YOUR PROMISES. THANK YOU! AMEN.

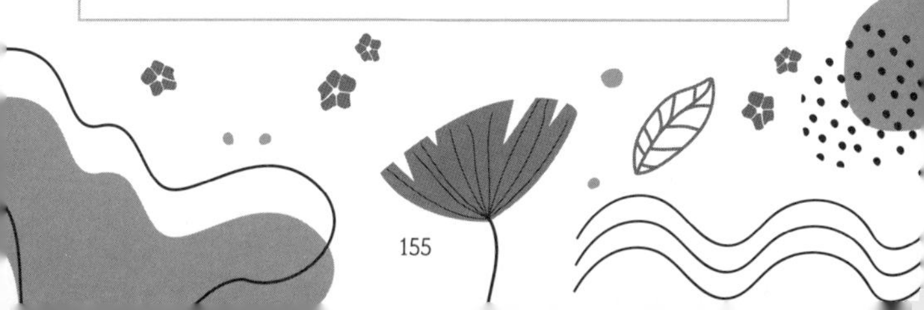

SIN LEADS TO DESTRUCTION

Blessed is the one who does not walk in step with the wicked or stand in the way that sinners take or sit in the company of mockers, but whose delight is in the law of the LORD, and who meditates on his law day and night. . . . Therefore the wicked will not stand in the judgment, nor sinners in the assembly of the righteous. For the LORD watches over the way of the righteous, but the way of the wicked leads to destruction.

PSALM 1:1–2, 5–6 NIV

In your teenage and young adult years, the world will tell you how fun it is to play around with sin and risky behavior. But the world lies. God's Word tells you to run away from the evil desires of youth and pursue righteousness, faith, love, and peace instead (2 Timothy 2:22).

Watch even a few minutes of the daily news. Do you really want to trust this crazy, broken world and experiment with sin, or do you want to trust the never-changing God who gives you life and your every breath—the one who loves you so much He even sent His only Son to die for you?

DEAR LORD, PLEASE HELP ME TO STAND STRONG IN MY LOVE FOR YOU, IN MY FAITH, AND IN MY OBEDIENCE TO YOU. REMIND ME OF YOUR DEEP LOVE AND GREAT SACRIFICE TO PAY FOR MY SIN SO THAT I WILL NEVER WANT TO PLAY AROUND WITH SIN. AMEN.

THE TRUSTWORTHY WORD OF GOD

We also thank God continually because, when you received the word of God, which you heard from us, you accepted it not as a human word, but as it actually is, the word of God, which is indeed at work in you who believe.

1 Thessalonians 2:13 NIV

Do you ever stop and wonder, or has anyone ever asked you, "How do I know the Bible is true? Why should I trust it?" If you take time to look, you will find amazing research from experts throughout history who verify why the Bible can be trusted far more than any other book ever written. More importantly, you can remember that you have a relationship with God Himself through Jesus Christ, and you have the Holy Spirit in you.

As you read the Bible consistently over time, ask God to show you more about Himself to you through His Word. Ask Him to grow your faith, and then trust Him to do it! You will be amazed at how He answers your prayers.

HEAVENLY FATHER, PLEASE KEEP GROWING MY FAITH IN YOU AS I READ YOUR AWESOME WORD! SHOW ME HOW AND WHY IT'S TRUE AND CAN BE TRUSTED. AMEN.

BE BOLD ABOUT JESUS

The Jewish leaders tried to find [Jesus] at the festival and kept asking if anyone had seen him. There was a lot of grumbling about him among the crowds. Some argued, "He's a good man," but others said, "He's nothing but a fraud who deceives the people." But no one had the courage to speak favorably about him in public, for they were afraid of getting in trouble with the Jewish leaders.

JOHN 7:11–13 NLT

When Jesus was teaching on earth, some people who heard Him thought He was a good man, but they kept quiet because they were afraid. They didn't want to get in trouble with the Jewish leaders who were saying Jesus was a liar and a fake. Learn from this, and ask God to help you never to be afraid of anyone who says Jesus is a fake. Those people might seem powerful in this world, but they are never more powerful than God. They are never more powerful than the good plans He has for you when you stay close to Him and stand strong in your faith.

Be bold and speak up for Jesus and bravely tell others about Him, how He has saved you, and all the good things He is doing in your life.

I AM PROUD OF YOU, JESUS! I WANT TO BE BOLD ABOUT YOU! I NEVER WANT TO FEAR ANYONE WHO DENIES YOU! YOU ARE MY SAVIOR, AND I LOVE YOU! AMEN.

CONQUERING FEARS, PART 1

When I am afraid, I will put my trust in you. I praise God for what he has promised. I trust in God, so why should I be afraid?

Psalm 56:3–4 NLT

Think about a fear you used to have but then you overcame it. How did God help you? Who were the people and what were the ways God provided to get you through it? It's so good to take quiet time occasionally, to focus on things you used to be afraid of that now seem like no big deal. It helps you realize that whatever is making you scared today will probably one day soon also be no big deal.

God never leaves you alone. He is right there with you in the middle of your fears, and you can call out for His help at any time. He will guide you through it to the other side where you can look back with relief and say, "Thanks, God! We conquered that together, and now I'm not afraid anymore!"

ALMIGHTY GOD, PLEASE HELP ME WITH THESE FEARS I HAVE: ________________. I REMEMBER ALL THE WAYS YOU HAVE HELPED ME GET OVER FEARS IN THE PAST, AND I AM TRUSTING THAT YOU WILL DO IT AGAIN. AMEN.

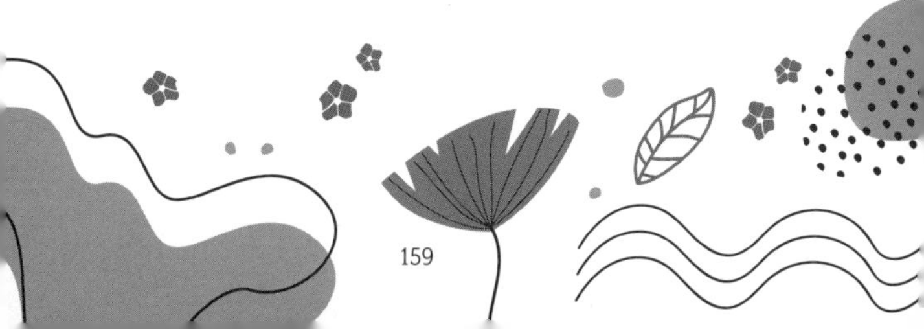

CONQUERING FEARS, PART 2

Even though I walk through the valley of the shadow of death, I will fear no evil, for you are with me; your rod and your staff, they comfort me.

PSALM 23:4 ESV

When you're working on conquering a fear, draw close to God through His Word and through prayer and praise. In your quiet time today, focus on scriptures about fear like these and repeat them, pray them, and sing them:

- "The Lord is my light and the One Who saves me. Whom should I fear? The Lord is the strength of my life. Of whom should I be afraid?" (Psalm 27:1 NLV).
- "God is our refuge and strength, an ever-present help in trouble. Therefore we will not fear, though the earth give way and the mountains fall into the heart of the sea" (Psalm 46:1–2 NIV).

When your mind is focused on God, it doesn't have room to focus on fear.

DEAR GOD, WHEN I FEEL AFRAID, PLEASE HELP ME TO KEEP MY MIND THINKING ABOUT YOU AND YOUR WORD. KEEP ME PRAYING TO YOU AND PRAISING YOU. AMEN.

SOMETIMES FEAR IS GOOD

Wise choices will watch over you. Understanding will keep you safe. Wisdom will save you from evil people, from those whose words are twisted. These men turn from the right way to walk down dark paths.

PROVERBS 2:11–13 NLT

Not all fear is bad. Sometimes fear can be good for you when it keeps you out of danger and trouble. For example, you don't have to fear a backyard campfire, but you should fear fire in the way that you know you should never play around with it and cause damage. Another example: you should fear what would happen if you were to listen to some friends who want you to join them in doing unwise things. That's a good fear to pay attention to, because you don't want to suffer the consequences of doing something stupid or dangerous.

God can use fear to keep you away from what would be harmful or foolish for you, so keep on asking Him to show you the times when it's good to listen to fear.

DEAR GOD, PLEASE HELP ME TO KNOW WHEN FEAR IS GOOD FOR ME BECAUSE YOU'RE USING IT TO KEEP ME SAFE. THANK YOU FOR WATCHING OVER ME SO WELL! AMEN.

ARE YOU TRYING TO KEEP SECRETS?

The eyes of the Lord are in every place,
watching the bad and the good.

PROVERBS 15:3 NLV

Are there any secrets you're trying to keep from God? We all need to ask ourselves this sometimes. We might think we can hide things we've done wrong, but it's just not true. We need to remember that God sees and knows everything all the time. Focusing on this truth can help us avoid sin. God is always going to see our sin, and there will be consequences. Thankfully, He loves to forgive us, like 1 John 1:9 (NLV) says: "If we tell Him our sins, He is faithful and we can depend on Him to forgive us of our sins. He will make our lives clean from all sin."

HELP ME TO TRULY APPRECIATE THAT I CAN'T KEEP SECRETS FROM YOU, LORD. THAT MEANS YOU ARE ALWAYS WATCHING ME BECAUSE YOU CARE ABOUT ME AND WANT TO KEEP ME OUT OF TROUBLE.

JESUS TAUGHT US NOT TO WORRY

"That is why I tell you not to worry about everyday life—whether you have enough food and drink, or enough clothes to wear. Isn't life more than food, and your body more than clothing? Look at the birds. They don't plant or harvest or store food in barns, for your heavenly Father feeds them. And aren't you far more valuable to him than they are? Can all your worries add a single moment to your life? . . . So don't worry about these things, saying, 'What will we eat? What will we drink? What will we wear?' These things dominate the thoughts of unbelievers, but your heavenly Father already knows all your needs. Seek the Kingdom of God above all else, and live righteously, and he will give you everything you need."

MATTHEW 6:25–27, 31–33 NLT

"No worries," we often say, and we can truly mean it when we trust in Jesus. In your quiet time today, focus on His teaching about why we shouldn't worry.

DEAR JESUS, PLEASE HELP ME TO REMEMBER THAT YOU HAVE SAID I SHOULDN'T WORRY ABOUT ANYTHING WHEN I'M TRUSTING MY LIFE TO YOU. AMEN.

LET GOD'S WORD LIGHT YOUR WAY

How sweet is Your Word to my taste! It is sweeter than honey to my mouth! I get understanding from Your Law and so I hate every false way. Your Word is a lamp to my feet and a light to my path. I have promised that I will keep Your Law. And I will add strength to this promise. . . . My life is always in my hand, yet I do not forget Your Law. The sinful have set a trap for me, yet I have not turned from Your Law. I have been given Your Law forever. It is the joy of my heart. I have set my heart on obeying Your Law forever, even to the end.

Psalm 119:103–106, 109–112 NLV

Is God's Word what is really, truly lighting your path and leading the way in your life? He wants us all to love His Word and find joy in following it because it's our guidebook for the best kind of life, with blessings and rewards both now and forever.

DEAR GOD, HELP ME TO LOVE YOUR WORD AND TO FOLLOW IT MORE CLOSELY EACH DAY OF MY LIFE AS I GROW IN RELATIONSHIP WITH YOU. AMEN.

DON'T EVER GIVE UP ON THE ONE TRUE GOD

I waited patiently for the LORD; he turned to me and heard my cry. He lifted me out of the slimy pit, out of the mud and mire; he set my feet on a rock and gave me a firm place to stand. He put a new song in my mouth, a hymn of praise to our God. Many will see and fear the LORD and put their trust in him. Blessed is the one who trusts in the LORD, who does not look to the proud, to those who turn aside to false gods.

PSALM 40:1–4 NIV

Even when times are hard, even when you feel like you've been waiting forever, don't give up on God. He *will* come through. He will rescue you from trouble. He will give you joy and encouragement. And on top of that, He will let others see your faith in Him, and they will come to love and follow God too.

I DON'T EVER WANT TO GIVE UP ON YOU, LORD, BECAUSE YOU LOVE ME AND NEVER GIVE UP ON ME. THANK YOU! AMEN.

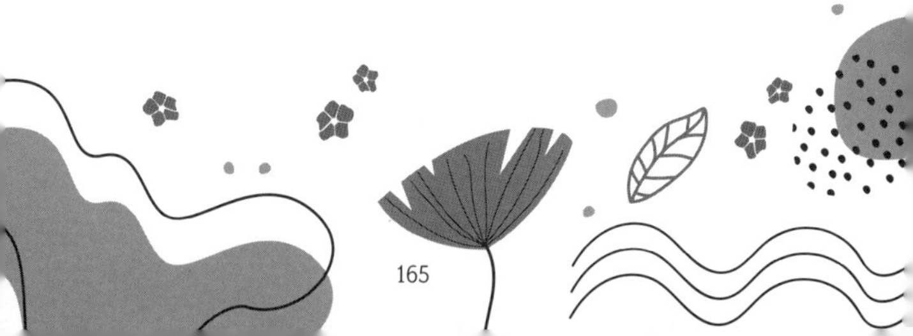

WHEN YOU SERVE THE LEAST OF THESE

"Then the righteous will answer him, saying, 'Lord, when did we see you hungry and feed you, or thirsty and give you drink? And when did we see you a stranger and welcome you, or naked and clothe you? And when did we see you sick or in prison and visit you?' And the King will answer them, 'Truly, I say to you, as you did it to one of the least of these my brothers, you did it to me.'"

MATTHEW 25:37–40 ESV

Jesus taught that whenever those who love Him help someone in need, it's like we're helping Jesus Himself. So, in your quiet time today, think about someone in your life who is needy right now. What can you do and give to help and encourage that person? If you can't think of anyone, ask God to show you who He wants you to help and the best ways to do so.

DEAR JESUS, THANK YOU THAT I CAN SERVE YOU AND SHOW MY LOVE TO YOU BY SERVING OTHERS. AMEN.

YOU WON'T BE SHAKEN

Give all your cares to the Lord and He will give you strength. He will never let those who are right with Him be shaken.

Psalm 55:22 NLV

Life feels scary and unsure sometimes, but God promises that those who are right with Him will never be shaken. (Remember: you are right with Him when you've asked Jesus to take away your sin and be your Savior.) Is there something you feel scared or uncertain or weak about today? Let God take those things away from you and give you His peace and power instead. First Peter 5:7 (NLV) says, "Give all your worries to Him because He cares for you." Our heavenly Father is so loving that He literally doesn't want us to worry about a thing! We can trust Him to take care of it all.

DEAR GOD, I DON'T KNOW WHY I HOLD ON TO WORRIES SO OFTEN, FOR YOU'VE TOLD ME YOU WANT TO TAKE THEM AWAY FROM ME. PLEASE HELP ME TO GET BETTER AT THIS. I WANT TO TRUST YOU MORE AND HAVE MORE OF YOUR PERFECT PEACE AND POWER. AMEN.

DON'T HATE DISCIPLINE

God's discipline is always good for us, so that we might share in his holiness. No discipline is enjoyable while it is happening—it's painful! But afterward there will be a peaceful harvest of right living for those who are trained in this way.

HEBREWS 12:10–11 NLT

When you get in trouble, do you instantly think of your punishment as something to be grateful for? Probably not. But if you think about what the Bible says about punishment and discipline, you can choose to see the good. Adults in your life are truly helping you when they punish or discipline you in wise ways for things you've done wrong. They're trying to teach you safety, honesty, respect, and responsibility.

In your quiet time today, ask God for wisdom and to help you appreciate punishment and discipline, even if you hate them at first. Choose to learn from them and let God show you how He is maturing and teaching you through discipline.

HEAVENLY FATHER, PLEASE HELP ME WHEN I'VE DONE SOMETHING WRONG AND THEN HAVE TO FACE THE CONSEQUENCES. EVEN THOUGH I DON'T ENJOY IT, I WANT TO BE ABLE TO APPRECIATE WISE PUNISHMENT AND DISCIPLINE, BOTH NOW AND IN THE FUTURE. AMEN.

EQUAL IN CHRIST JESUS

For you are all children of God through faith in Christ Jesus. And all who have been united with Christ in baptism have put on Christ, like putting on new clothes. There is no longer Jew or Gentile, slave or free, male and female. For you are all one in Christ Jesus. And now that you belong to Christ, you are the true children of Abraham. You are his heirs, and God's promise to Abraham belongs to you.

GALATIANS 3:26–29 NLT

In your quiet time today, ask God to teach you about real equality. Because of sin in the world, people will never get equality exactly right here on earth. There will always be terrible people trying to say some groups of people are better than others. Ignore them. In God's eyes, every single person is the same in value. We matter so much to God that He sent Jesus to die to save us from our sins. And when anyone trusts in Jesus, they become a child of the one true God, the King of all kings. That makes all followers of Jesus equal in royalty, and we should want to share that awesome truth with everyone we can!

HEAVENLY FATHER, YOU OFFER THE ONLY TRUE EQUALITY THROUGH JESUS. THANK YOU THAT ANYONE CAN BE YOUR CHILD BY TRUSTING THAT ONLY JESUS SAVES. AMEN.

DON'T KEEP ON SINNING

Are we to keep on sinning so that God will give us more of His loving-favor? No, not at all! We are dead to sin. How then can we keep on living in sin?

ROMANS 6:1–2 NLV

When we ask God for forgiveness from sin, He forgives so fully and so well! So sometimes we might think it's no big deal to keep sinning and then just keep asking for more forgiveness. But if we truly love God, we want to obey Him and honor Him, not choose sin again and again with a "who cares?" attitude.

We are going to mess up and make bad choices sometimes, but we should feel sincerely sorry about our sin and how it hurts God. Then we should do our best not to sin in the future. Also, even though God always forgives when we ask, He doesn't always keep us from the consequences of sin. Ask God to help you keep running away from sin, not playing around with it like it doesn't matter.

DEAR GOD, I KNOW THAT YOU LOVE ME NO MATTER WHAT, BUT I DON'T WANT TO SIN AGAINST YOU ON PURPOSE AND PRETEND IT'S NO BIG DEAL. PLEASE HELP ME TO KEEP GROWING IN WISDOM ABOUT YOUR WONDERFUL GRACE. AMEN.

THROUGH MANY TRIALS

So be truly glad. There is wonderful joy ahead, even though you must endure many trials for a little while. These trials will show that your faith is genuine. It is being tested as fire tests and purifies gold—though your faith is far more precious than mere gold. So when your faith remains strong through many trials, it will bring you much praise and glory and honor on the day when Jesus Christ is revealed to the whole world. You love him even though you have never seen him. Though you do not see him now, you trust him; and you rejoice with a glorious, inexpressible joy. The reward for trusting him will be the salvation of your souls.

1 Peter 1:6–9 NLT

Even during hard times, we can have joy. Hard times are tests that show whether our faith in Jesus is real or fake. It's easy to say we love and trust Jesus when we have no problems, but keeping faith during hard times shows that we *truly* trust in Him.

EVEN WHEN LIFE IS HARD, AND EVEN THOUGH I DON'T SEE YOU IN PERSON, JESUS, I WILL KEEP ON TRUSTING YOU. MY FAITH IN YOU IS REAL, NOT FAKE. AMEN.

IN GOD'S HANDS

But I trust in you, Lord; I say, "You are my God." My times are in your hands.

Psalm 31:14–15 niv

When you think about the future, it might be overwhelming. How do you know which path or college or job to choose? And then there are relationships. Who to be friends with, who to date, who to marry someday. . . It's a lot to think about!

First, trust that you are God's masterpiece. He created you "in Christ Jesus, so [you] can do the good things he planned for [you] long ago" (Ephesians 2:10 nlt). And then remember that all your times, every moment of every day, are in God's hands. You don't have to figure everything out right now. Dream and pray about your future, and then give it all to God. Constantly ask Him for His will to be done in your life and trust Him and let Him lead you day by day.

LORD, YOU ARE MY GOD, AND I'M SO GLAD AND GRATEFUL THAT MY TIMES ARE IN YOUR HANDS. THANK YOU FOR CREATING ME WITH PURPOSE. I WANT YOUR WILL AND YOUR PLANS FOR MY LIFE. I'LL KEEP TRUSTING THAT YOU'LL LEAD ME, SHOW ME, AND HELP ME. AMEN.

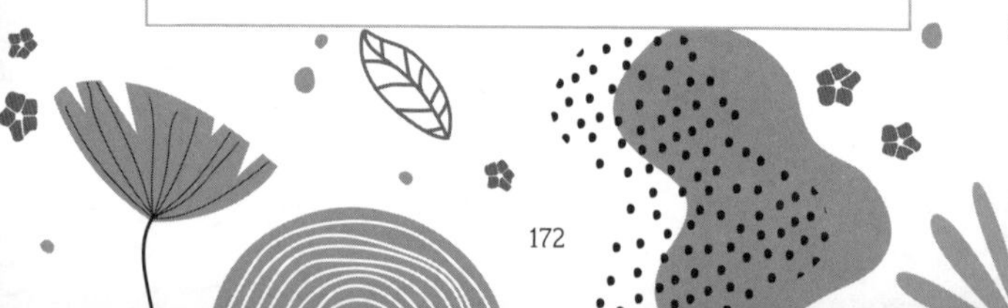

WHAT WE CAN'T SEE YET

That is why we never give up. Though our bodies are dying, our spirits are being renewed every day. For our present troubles are small and won't last very long. Yet they produce for us a glory that vastly outweighs them and will last forever! So we don't look at the troubles we can see now; rather, we fix our gaze on things that cannot be seen. For the things we see now will soon be gone, but the things we cannot see will last forever.

2 Corinthians 4:16–18 NLT

The troubles of life can feel awful and overwhelming, especially when they pile up. So we must remember that the Bible says that every trouble we go through now is getting us ready for the best things God has for us forever. Someday in heaven we'll go through no troubles at all. If we focus our thoughts on all the wonderful things we can't see yet—the things God has promised—we'll get through the hard things that are part of our lives right now.

DEAR GOD, I'M EXCITED FOR THE GOOD THINGS YOU'RE GOING TO GIVE FOREVER TO ALL WHO LOVE AND TRUST IN YOU. I WANT TO FOCUS ON THOSE THINGS AS YOU HELP ME TO GET THROUGH EARTHLY TROUBLES TODAY. AMEN.

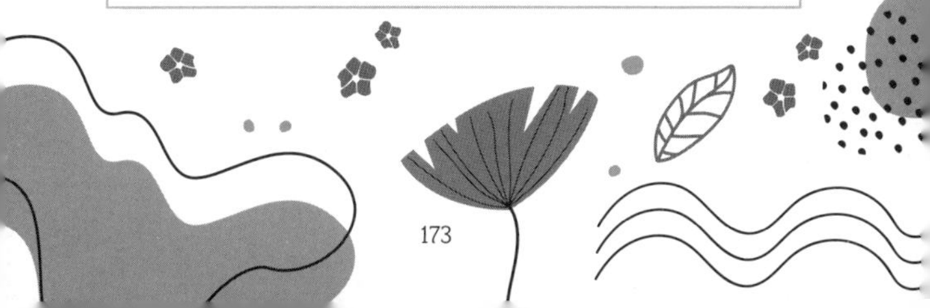

AWESOME GOD

The word of the Lord holds true, and we can trust everything he does. He loves whatever is just and good; the unfailing love of the Lord fills the earth. The Lord merely spoke, and the heavens were created. He breathed the word, and all the stars were born. He assigned the sea its boundaries and locked the oceans in vast reservoirs. Let the whole world fear the Lord, and let everyone stand in awe of him. For when he spoke, the world began! It appeared at his command. The Lord frustrates the plans of the nations and thwarts all their schemes. But the Lord's plans stand firm forever; his intentions can never be shaken. What joy for the nation whose God is the Lord, whose people he has chosen as his inheritance.

Psalm 33:4–12 NLT

Focus on God's greatness in your quiet time today, like this psalm describes. God is more awesome than we can possibly imagine! There is nothing and no one like almighty God. Nothing can stop Him and His perfect plans. And all who belong to Him are blessed forever!

ALMIGHTY GOD, YOU ARE AWESOME, AND I'M BLESSED TO BE YOUR CHILD. AMEN.

BE REAL

Don't just pretend to love others. Really love them. Hate what is wrong. Hold tightly to what is good. Love each other with genuine affection, and take delight in honoring each other.

ROMANS 12:9–10 NLT

You probably know people who seem fake. They say nice things some of the time, but they do mean things a lot of the time. They say things that are kind and loving, but they don't truly act kind and loving. When we deal with these people, we should learn lessons on how *not* to be. We should want to be real and sincere, honest and genuine, in everything we do.

Yes, we'll mess up sometimes, and we'll need grace, but we should always be trying our best never to be fake. We shouldn't pretend to love others—we should truly love them with God's love.

DEAR GOD, PLEASE FORGIVE ME FOR THE TIMES I'VE LIED AND BEEN DISHONEST AND FAKE WITH MY WORDS AND ACTIONS TOWARD OTHERS. FILL ME WITH REAL LOVE—YOUR LOVE. AMEN.

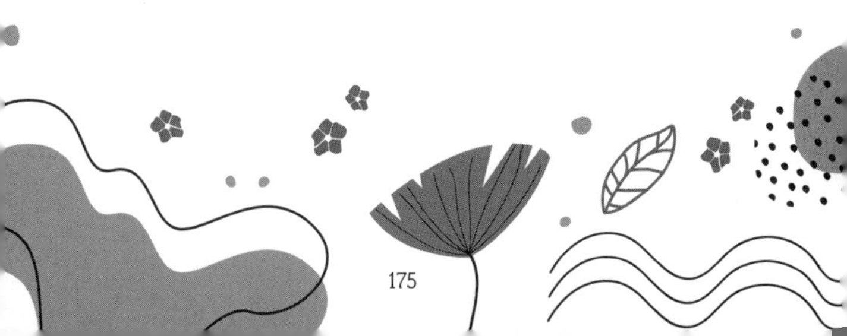

ONLY ONE SAID THANKS

Ten men with a bad skin disease came to Him. . . .
They called to Him, "Jesus! Teacher! Take pity on us!"
When Jesus saw them, He said, "Go and show yourselves
to the religious leaders." As they went, they were healed.
One of them turned back when he saw he was healed.
He thanked God with a loud voice. He got down on his
face at the feet of Jesus and thanked Him. . . . Jesus
asked, "Were there not ten men who were healed?
Where are the other nine? Is this stranger from
another country the only one who turned back to give
thanks to God?" Then Jesus said to him, "Get up and
go on your way. Your trust in God has healed you."

LUKE 17:12–19 NLV

Ten men had been miraculously healed by Jesus. You'd think they would have been extremely excited and grateful to Him. Yet only one of them turned back to Jesus to thank Him and worship Him.

In whatever ways God blesses us, we should always want to be like the one man and not the other nine! So spend some quiet time today thanking God for many specific ways He has provided for you and blessed you.

I DON'T EVER WANT TO FORGET TO GIVE YOU THANKS FOR ALL YOU DO FOR ME, LORD! I AM GRATEFUL, AND I WANT TO WORSHIP AND PRAISE YOU AT ALL TIMES FOR EVERYTHING. AMEN.

DON'T GET WEARY

Let us not become weary in doing good, for at the proper time we will reap a harvest if we do not give up. Therefore, as we have opportunity, let us do good to all people, especially to those who belong to the family of believers.

GALATIANS 6:9–10 NIV

Sometimes we feel like giving up on doing the right thing. We watch people who never help others and who break the rules and do bad things seeming to live good lives without getting caught or punished—and that can discourage us. It can tempt us to do the same thing or to get depressed.

So we must remember that God's Word tells us not to get tired and weary of doing good. If we don't give up on following Jesus, God will bless us at exactly the right time with exactly the things He knows we need and will give us true, forever joy.

I NEED YOUR HELP NEVER TO GET WEARY OF FOLLOWING YOUR WORD AND YOUR WAYS, LORD. PLEASE ENCOURAGE ME AND REMIND ME THAT THE MAIN REASON I DO GOOD THINGS IS TO MAKE YOU HAPPY BECAUSE YOU LOVE ME MORE THAN ANYONE, AND I WANT TO OBEY YOU TO SHOW MY LOVE BACK TO YOU. AMEN.

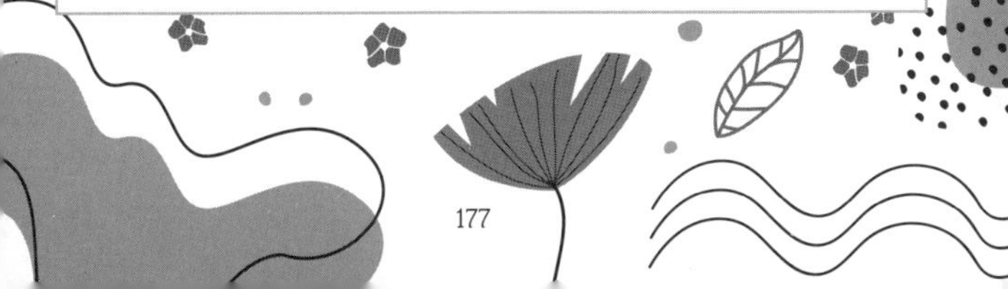

GOD NEVER WEARS OUT

Do you not know? Have you not heard? The LORD is the everlasting God, the Creator of the ends of the earth. He will not grow tired or weary, and his understanding no one can fathom. He gives strength to the weary and increases the power of the weak. Even youths grow tired and weary, and young men stumble and fall; but those who hope in the LORD will renew their strength. They will soar on wings like eagles; they will run and not grow weary, they will walk and not be faint.

ISAIAH 40:28–31 NIV

No matter how much energy we wake up with every day, it always runs out. Whether we like it or not, we must sleep. Only God can never get tired and never wears out. He's amazing! Yes, we need physical rest, but we also need to come to God in regular quiet time so that He can give us spiritual rest and a jolt of spiritual energy.

DEAR GOD, I PRAISE YOU FOR YOUR AWESOME, ENDLESS POWER, YOUR ENERGY THAT NEVER RUNS OUT! PLEASE GIVE ME SPIRITUAL STRENGTH AND ENERGY EACH DAY. AMEN.

DON'T EVER BE ASHAMED OF THE GOOD NEWS

I am not ashamed of the Good News. It is the power of God. It is the way He saves men from the punishment of their sins if they put their trust in Him. It is for the Jew first and for all other people also. The Good News tells us we are made right with God by faith in Him. Then, by faith we live that new life through Him.

Romans 1:16–17 NLV

Just as the apostle Paul shared in Romans 1, we should all want to be able to say this: we are not embarrassed or ashamed of the good news. The good news is that Jesus came to earth to live a perfect life and teach us, and He died on the cross to pay for our sins. Then He rose to life again, and He offers us eternal life too. When we share this good news with others, we help spread God's power to save people from their sins.

DEAR GOD, PLEASE HELP ME NEVER TO BE EMBARRASSED OR ASHAMED TO SHARE THE GOOD NEWS ABOUT JESUS! THANK YOU FOR LOVING ALL PEOPLE AND WANTING TO SAVE US ALL FROM SIN! AMEN.

KEEP LOOKING UP

I will lift up my eyes to the mountains. Where will my help come from? My help comes from the Lord, Who made heaven and earth. He will not let your feet go out from under you. He Who watches over you will not sleep. . . . The sun will not hurt you during the day and the moon will not hurt you during the night. The Lord will keep you from all that is sinful. He will watch over your soul. The Lord will watch over your coming and going, now and forever.

Psalm 121:1–3, 6–8 NLV

Whatever crazy things might be going on in your life, keep looking up to God in heaven. Stay positive and remember that God is where all your help comes from. And since He is the Creator of everything, since He holds the universe together, never sleeps, and always watches over you, you can feel totally strong and courageous for whatever hard, sad, or scary thing you might be dealing with.

ALMIGHTY GOD, PLEASE HELP ME TO KEEP LOOKING UP TOWARD YOU, ALWAYS LOOKING TO YOU FOR HELP AND HOPE. AMEN.

BE A GOOD LEADER AND MENTOR

In all things show them how to live by your life and by right teaching. You should be wise in what you say. Then the one who is against you will be ashamed and will not be able to say anything bad about you.

TITUS 2:7–8 NLV

In your quiet time today, think about how you are leading others. Someone younger is always looking up to you. So, are you being a good leader and mentor and setting a good example?

At school, at church, in your community, and in your activities, ask God to help you show the younger people in your life that you care about them. As you build friendships with those who are younger than you, you can become a great mentor to them and point them to Jesus as you keep following Him and they look up to and follow you.

DEAR GOD, I LOOK UP TO YOU FIRST. AND AS I ALSO LOOK UP TO AND FOLLOW GOOD AND WISE LEADERS AND MENTORS WHO LOVE YOU, HELP ME TO BE A GOOD LEADER AND MENTOR TO OTHERS TOO. AMEN.

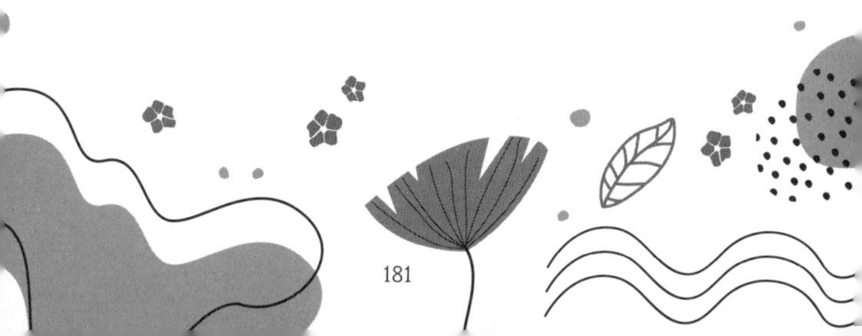

ONCE AND FOR ALL TIME

[Jesus] is holy and blameless, unstained by sin. He has been set apart from sinners and has been given the highest place of honor in heaven. Unlike those other high priests, he does not need to offer sacrifices every day. They did this for their own sins first and then for the sins of the people. But Jesus did this once for all when he offered himself as the sacrifice for the people's sins.

HEBREWS 7:26–27 NLT

All religions are not the same. Faith in Jesus is the only faith worth having. Jesus was the only human being to live on earth who was also holy and without any sin. He gave His own life to die once for all people of all time to save them from their sin. Then He rose again to show His power over death and offer forever life to all who trust in Him. No other religion offers such a gift of love.

To know Jesus as Savior is to believe in Him and accept His awesome gift of grace, for He took our sins away when He died on the cross and then rose to life again.

DEAR JESUS, THANK YOU FOR GIVING YOUR LIFE TO SAVE EVERYONE WHO BELIEVES IN YOU! THERE IS NO ONE ELSE LIKE YOU! YOU ARE GOD, AND YOU ARE THE ONE AND ONLY LIVING SAVIOR! AMEN.

WITH THE STRENGTH OF CHRIST

I can do all things through [Christ] who strengthens me.

PHILIPPIANS 4:13 ESV

Have you ever wanted to immediately quit something so, *so* badly? Maybe you wished you could drop out of a class at school because it was way too hard. Or maybe you tried a new sport but didn't want to finish the season. We've all been there.

But when we do complete a semester or a season without quitting, sometimes we can look back and see how God was giving us just the right amount of courage and strength and blessing to take things one day at a time—or even just one moment at a time! And hopefully we can see how He used that time to grow us into better, stronger people because we endured instead of giving up.

In any hard situation, call on God to help, and then trust in and wait on Him. He will either help you walk through it day by day until it's over or help you find a wise way out immediately.

FATHER GOD, PLEASE HELP ME WHEN I WANT TO QUIT IN A HARD SITUATION. PLEASE BLESS ME WITH POWERFUL STRENGTH, ENDURANCE, COURAGE, AND WISDOM. AMEN.

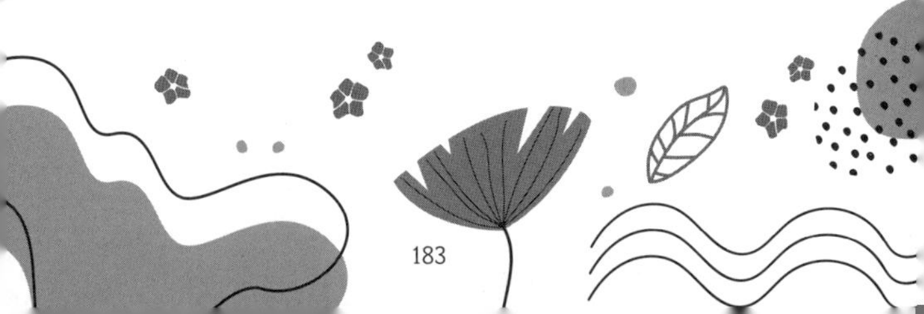

JUST FOR A WHILE

In his kindness God called you to share in his eternal glory by means of Christ Jesus. So after you have suffered a little while, he will restore, support, and strengthen you, and he will place you on a firm foundation. All power to him forever!

1 Peter 5:10–11 NLT

A perfect life here on earth would be nice. But we all know that's not possible. There are all kinds of troubles and hurts in this world—little ones like failing a test, and big ones like losing a loved one. But God's Word promises that all kinds of suffering and pain are just for a little while in this world as we wait for perfect paradise forever in heaven. Meanwhile, if we follow Him, God will keep us on the right path and give us joy, comfort, strength, and endurance to deal with the hard things of this life. None of them can ever overpower us as we depend on the one true God who has power over all of them.

HEAVENLY FATHER, I HATE THE HURT IN THIS WORLD, BUT I LOVE THAT YOU HAVE COMPLETE POWER OVER ALL OF IT. I TRUST THAT YOU ARE WORKING TO MAKE ALL THINGS PERFECT FOREVER IN HEAVEN—FOR ME AND ALL WHO TRUST IN YOUR SON, JESUS. AMEN.

WE CAN'T WORK OUR WAY TO GOD AND HEAVEN

People are counted as righteous, not because of their work, but because of their faith in God who forgives sinners.

ROMANS 4:5 NLT

We can't ever work our way to God's "good side" and into heaven. Imagine how exhausting that would be, how much anxiety we'd have wondering if we were doing a "good enough" job!

Thankfully, our salvation is a gift from God that we receive from Him because of our faith: we believe that God sent Jesus to pay the price for our sin, and we believe that Jesus died on the cross and rose again. We believe that the only way to heaven is through Jesus Christ. We admit our sin and ask God to forgive us for it. Then we let Jesus be Lord over our lives, doing our best to obey and follow His ways, which we learn from the Bible and the Holy Spirit guiding us.

HEAVENLY FATHER, THANK YOU THAT I CAN'T EVER WORK MY WAY TO HEAVEN. YOU NEVER EXPECTED ME TO. I COULD NEVER PAY THE PRICE FOR MY SIN ON MY OWN, SO YOU GAVE JESUS AS MY SAVIOR. I AM BEYOND GRATEFUL, AND I WANT TO LIVE ALL MY LIFE TO HONOR AND BRING PRAISE TO YOU. AMEN.

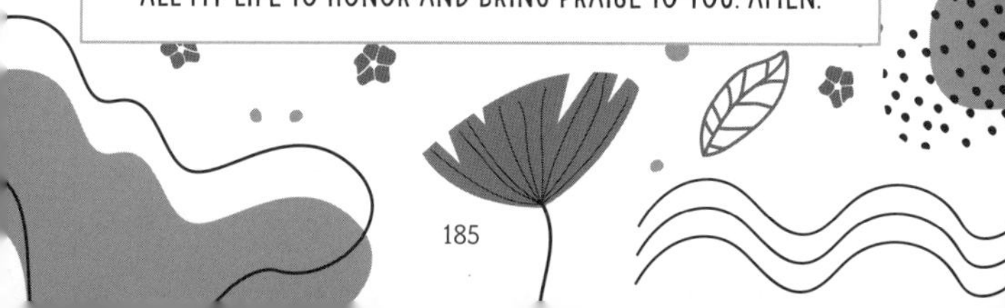

HOW TO HAVE PERFECT PEACE

You will keep in perfect peace all who trust in you, all whose thoughts are fixed on you! Trust in the Lord *always, for the* Lord God *is the eternal Rock. . . . For those who are righteous, the way is not steep and rough. You are a God who does what is right, and you smooth out the path ahead of them.* Lord, *we show our trust in you by obeying your laws; our heart's desire is to glorify your name. In the night I search for you; in the morning I earnestly seek you. For only when you come to judge the earth will people learn what is right.*

Isaiah 26:3–4, 7–9 NLT

Focus on perfect peace in your quiet time today. Perfect peace almost sounds *way* too good to be true, doesn't it?

There always seems to be something stressing us out, even if it's just a family squabble or an annoying classmate or a huge homework assignment. But God's Word tells us how to have perfect peace—by trusting in God and fixing our thoughts on Him. When we feel our peace being disrupted, we need to turn our attention back to God and ask for His help to handle what's causing the stress.

HEAVENLY FATHER, I TRUST YOU AND WOULD LOVE TO HAVE PERFECT PEACE ALL THE TIME. PLEASE HELP ME TO TURN MY THOUGHTS BACK TO YOU IN STRESSFUL SITUATIONS AND TO KEEP THEM THERE! AMEN.

SCRIPTURE INDEX

OLD TESTAMENT

NEW TESTAMENT